Once Upon a Reader

Once Upon a Reader

Raising Your Children With a Love of Books

LORRAINE LEVIS

CURRACH
BOOKS

First published in 2020 by

 **CURRACH**BOOKS

Block 3b, Bracken Business Park, Bracken Road
Sandyford, Dublin 18, D18 K277
www.currachbooks.com

ISBN: 978-1-78218-920-6

Second Print

Set in Adelle PE & Adelle Sans 11/15
Cover illustration by Alba Esteban
Book design by Alba Esteban | Currach Books
Text illustrations by Freepik
Printed by L&C Poland

To Mum and Dad

Contents

· ·

Introduction

First things first: thank you for opening this book. If you have, you are either my mother or you're curious about how best to introduce and maintain a love of reading in your child's life. If you're reading this book as someone who isn't really into reading yourself, thank you for picking it up. Making an effort to maximise your child's engagement with books is an amazing gift for you to give them. If you are trying to fall in love with reading for the first time, or looking to re-engage your own inner reader who has maybe been absent for a while, here are my tips for making it as easy as possible.

1 Forget about what everyone else has told you about their reading experiences

Everyone is different. There are lots of friends who like the same types of books but when it comes down to it, everyone's taste is unique to them. Just because one of your friends adores early twentieth-century Russian literature doesn't mean you need to like it too. Something they consider 'easy reading' could be quite challenging or just downright boring for you.

As someone who has a BA in English literature but who mainly reads children's books, I know that you are most definitely not alone or less cultured than someone else just because you like to read books that don't present an extreme challenge to get through. Which leads me to:

2 Take the term 'guilty pleasure' and throw it in the bin

And then take the bin out and set it on fire. In the same way that I encourage children to read the books that make them happy because reading for pleasure shouldn't be school, I recommend to adults that they find those books that make them happy and stick with them. There is nothing that annoys me more than when a person says an author is their 'guilty pleasure'. Why are you feeling guilty about liking something that makes you happy?! Are you hurting anyone? No. Is it going to make a difference in anyone else's life what book you enjoy reading? Heck no! A guilty pleasure is just something you like but that society has told you that you should feel bad about. Change your headspace – if you don't see it as something to be guilty about, you can start to change the perception around it!

3 Draw inspiration from your other hobbies

If reading hasn't been on your radar as a hobby for a while, ease yourself in and tie it in to the things you love to do. Find biographies of your favourite actors or musicians, look at the history of the cars you love or novels that are set in the locations of your fondest memories. Finding the hook which connects you to the book is a great way to start reading for pleasure. Most hobbies have dedicated magazines, which are also a great way to dip your toe in as well as furthering your knowledge of what you love! It also segues nicely into point number four:

4 Start small

Going from nothing to a full novel can seem like a daunting commitment of time and energy. I'm starting to get the feeling that I have more half-read books on my shelf that I haven't finished as ones that I have. Getting part of the way through a book and realising that you just don't like the writing style or themes can be extremely frustrating (as well as a waste of money unless you use the library, in which case try as many as you want), so if you're looking to start with a new genre or author, try to find some of their short stories or shorter books to ease you in gently.

There is an amazing series of books called 'quick reads' which are small, complete stories written by popular authors and designed to be read in one sitting or just as a taster of what they have to offer. There are also more books coming out where the story is told through poetry instead of blocks of text. This is not the poetry you read in school; it's a quick and extremely engaging way of experiencing a story.

5 Read every night ... or when you can

This is something I picked up from my mum. No matter how late it is or how early she has to be up, she has to read at least a couple of pages every night before she's able to turn off and go to sleep. Creating a routine as you wind down is a great way to make sure you keep cutting your way through a book. It's also a great way to cut down on your screen time before bed, letting you disconnect from your phone with something with less glare! If night time doesn't work for you, find another time during the day to get some reading in. There are always moments during the day that we are aimlessly scrolling or day dreaming, when we're waiting for our food to cook or sitting on a bus. Over time you'll notice that you're reaching for the book whenever you can and you'll suddenly realise you're hooked!

6 Make sure there's no other reason for your reluctance

Sometimes it's not just a case of lack of motivation to read that is putting you off. If you haven't had a recent eye exam, get one to make sure that you don't need reading glasses; if you already wear glasses, check that your prescription is correct. You should also consider the idea that you might have an undiagnosed condition such as dyslexia, which might not have been noticed when you were in school. It's never too late to be assessed and there are a lot of resources for adults who need them. See Chapter 3 and www.dyslexia.ie for more information.

How to use this book

The next important thing is how I recommend you use this book and that's where the big disclaimer is ... THERE IS NO RIGHT WAY TO USE THIS BOOK.

When I decided I wanted to write the book I had a think about what the purpose was. I knew I wanted something informative but, as a woman with no children, I didn't want to try and tell people how to parent. As the closest thing I have to having any qualification in child psychology or anything like it is being very close to a child mentally myself, I knew I needed to bring something that was specific to me.

I'm hoping you will find this book informative for whatever stage your children are at, but I also want you to be able to read some of the other sections too. Children's literature is an amazing and ever-changing field, while also being so full of nostalgia that you feel you need to share it with those who come next. Because of that I want this book to help you to revisit some of your own memories of reading and also have a bit of a laugh with me as I share some of the lessons I've learned while working in this very specific form of specialised retail. Of course, if you don't have fond memories of reading when you were young, then I want to thank you even more for picking up this book. Making a commitment to promoting a love of reading when you don't have one yourself is admirable, and I really hope I can help bridge the gap for you.

This book starts with the baby stuff and ends with letting your young adults into areas of books that you don't need to help them with. More than anything, I want to start a dialogue between you and the children in your lives.

At the end of the day, it is you who is going to be the bridge between their world of innocence and that of the 'grown-ups', and that's a role that demands to be taken seriously. To make the transition between child and adult as smooth as possible you need to be tactful, respectful and, most importantly, you need to be there for them. I'm sure most of us can remember plainly which side of the line our parents were on in this regard but that doesn't mean you have to know everything all the time – that's where books come in.

Because new books are always being published, they are an amazing way to keep up with your children's lives as well as being a window onto the world as it must look to them. Literature tends to mimic the world in which it's published, so if you're finding it hard to figure out what they're thinking, have a look at the books they're reading, or what's top of the charts or trending online. You can be sure of gaining some insight into their minds that way, even if it is just full of vampires and vloggers!

In the end, what I really hope you gain from this book is a bit more confidence in knowing what your child needs or wants when it comes to their reading lives. I want you to be able to find that place of acceptance where you know what your child loves to read, even if you would rather it were something else; I want you to be able to see the value in their choice. I hope I can help you find that 'click moment' with your child, where they find exactly what they want and the joy of reading just 'clicks' with them, because that's a bug that's hard to get rid of and will delight them throughout their lives.

I hope I can help relieve some of the stress of gift-picking for holidays and birthdays because even if you love reading the maze of shelves in a bookshop can be daunting; it's hard enough to pick a book for yourself, let alone someone else! If this book can help you navigate the shelves while also helping you to understand what you're looking at, my job here is done!

Of course, you might disagree with me on some things and that's fine, not everyone is going to do everything exactly the same. I hope that my experiences of working with children to help them love reading will make you think about things a bit differently and help you remember that at the core of everything I have written here, the message is simple: reading is for everyone!

Finding the Perfect Book

Going into the children's department of any bookshop or library should be a joyful and positive experience for everyone, adults included. Unfortunately, like many other shopping experiences, it can also be completely overwhelming when you're looking for something specific. Add time and budget constraints and those colourful shelves full of new ideas and possibilities soon become an impenetrable wall of confusion and frustration.

This chapter is a handy cheat sheet to help you navigate the maze of different age ranges and topics so you can find the perfect choice for the little one in your life – and hopefully keep your sanity intact too!

1 Talk to a bookseller/librarian

I need to lay out a truth here. Your child, the light of your life and the centre of your universe, in many ways is exactly the same as most other children on this planet. Even if they are interested in what seems to be the most obscure topic, odds are that the person working in the book-based establishment you are searching in has probably dealt with these criteria before. Even if you have only the most basic idea of what you are looking for, they can give you a perspective you may not have considered and it will save you an awful lot of time staring at the shelves!

However, before you get to the point of being in the actual bookshop/library, please read point 2!

2 Do your research

This is especially important if you don't know the child you're buying for, but you would be surprised how many parents I've encountered who were unable to answer some simple questions that really make it easier to help pick a suitable book! Simply knowing if the child is a boy or a girl might not always cut it! Here are some of the basics that you should try to figure out, as they are the go-to questions I would ask a grown-up looking to pick out a kids' book:

How old is the child?

Simply knowing roughly what age you're working with can narrow things down significantly. If you aim too young, you run the risk of insulting the child by giving them a 'baby book' that they wouldn't be caught dead reading. Aim too old and the content of the book might not be suitable or they simply might not be able to read it because the words are too difficult. Getting past this first hurdle, even if you know rough ages, is the first step to book-buying success!

Boy or girl?

There is an argument to be made that gender shouldn't matter when it comes to picking books for children. I know a good number of children's booksellers, some of them are the best in the business, who would never ask the question in the first place. It could be argued that even asking, 'Is it for a boy or a girl?' could result in books being recommended that just aren't suitable for the child in question.

From a bookseller's perspective, it's easier to let the customer use the child's pronouns to determine gender and then follow with other questions that will elicit more specific answers. This isn't a political statement; it just makes sense that not every girl wants to read books that are pink, sparkly and about cute animals, and not all boys want to read about farts and dirt! If they do, that's great, but none of these are exclusive to gender and there's no point in pretending they are. Consider this:

> The scene is set. Our hero has travelled to the ends of the earth to find the cure to the devastating plague that has taken hold of the world. This cure will save lives and as he scoops the pure liquid out of the magic fountain, he siphons it into a random juice bottle he happens to have in his bag. He brings it to the people and there is uproar. People are screaming is dismay, holding their children and weeping.
>
> 'What's wrong?' the hero asks, confused by their reaction to the one thing that will save them.
>
> 'You've doomed half of the population by what you've done!'
>
> The hero is confused; the potion is strong enough to be diluted and distributed to all. 'Don't you see? How can we give this to the boys when there's a girl on the label?'

The ideas of gender are very deep rooted and are difficult to approach lightly. To limit your boys to diggers and dinosaurs and your girls to princesses and ponies, is to narrow their perspective - the exact opposite of what you're trying to do by encouraging them to read. At the same time, trying to keep girls away from 'girl things' and boys away from 'boy things' as a way to subvert what the world is trying to push on them, does exactly the same thing.

I usually find that boys (and their parents) are more reluctant to entertain a book with a female main character than the other way around. This conversation comes about mainly when they reach the independent reading stage and they have developed their own tastes. Many parents assume that they have developed a taste for books to which they can relate and that have characters whose gender they can identify with. I believe that the mindset that brings them to that point occurs much earlier on. Adults who come in to buy a book for a small child arrive with a basket of thoughts, dreams and expectations. These are coloured by their own experiences and the way they see the world. For good or ill, we are all in some way moulded by our experiences. Where someone has been raised to have a certain perception of what is suitable for boys and what is suitable for girls, because abiding by gender-based rules has produced happy outcomes, it is only natural that they want to present that safe view of the world to their child.

This becomes evident in the books they want to buy; strong, bold stories of boys being boys, full of energy and ready to take on the world. Whereas the girls' world is bright and lovely place, where problems are easily solved when the right thing is done, and friendship and kindness always prevail. There is nothing wrong with either of these approaches, but why can't they be transferable without being 'subversive' or 'brave'? If we can have children who can relate to a dinosaur who needs the potty or a unicorn who's lost its mum, why is it such a hard stretch for them to relate to another child who just happens to be the opposite gender? Promoting an 'us' and 'them' culture ensures that the adults they grow into will have the same deep-rooted preconceptions that the people who made those early decisions had and they will have to work to get beyond them. By introducing a range of books featuring children of different genders, races, abilities and family types, you ensure that they're getting the best chance of understanding the world you're preparing them for.

There is a theory that is quite prevalent in the children's book industry, especially amongst booksellers, which is that 'boys books are for everyone and girl's books are for girls', basically stating that the books with male protagonists are the default. For example, you would never tell a girl that she shouldn't read *Harry Potter* because she is a girl and Harry is a boy. However, it is unlikely that boys would be encouraged to read a magical realism series such as Jessica Townsend's *Nevermoor*.

When I was a teen and *Twilight* was all the rage I was working in a bookshop part time. I became flustered when a parent was in buying the third book and I presumed that the teen they were buying for was female. I quickly apologised and spouted on about how great it was that he was reading them and how more boys should. Thinking back, why did I do that?

The main character is a girl but there are plenty of male characters in the series. Did I seriously believe that there was something inherently brave about the fact that a boy was reading a romantic fantasy series that was supposedly for girls? It's only now that I'm writing this down that I realised that the person I was speaking to was the reader's father, not the reader. There is a strong possibility that the child sent the parent in to buy a book that wasn't intended for them, although adults had spent years telling them that the world is their oyster and that they could be who they wanted. There's a caveat at the end of that – so long as you play by the rules. That young man could have been terrified of being seen buying the book or being judged or laughed at by the person behind the till. That wouldn't have happened, but even I, as a bookseller, was ill equipped to deal with the fact that my presumption about who wanted the book was wrong.

We spend so much time driving home the idea that books are for everyone and that you should never be judged for what you enjoy reading. It is important to consider why you think about gender roles the way you do. It might be easier in your eyes for your child to fit into society's idea of what a boy and a girl should be, but if your child doesn't fit that mould, that is the fault of society, not the child. Having small children read only about their own gender isn't going to change anything, and will limit the amazing stories they could experience. Your role in their lives is to broaden their horizons, not narrow them. Keep that in mind the next time your little boy wants to read about princesses or your little girl wants a book about trucks: books are books and reading is reading – let them discover the world with you and you might end up learning a thing or two yourself!

Do they enjoy reading?

This question isn't designed to challenge why you came into the shop/library. No bookseller/librarian has ever asked this question, gotten a no for an answer and then told a customer to get out of the shop/library! Knowing if the child is a big reader tells us a lot. If they are, it means that they might be very up to date with what is new, so they should be given something that either came out that week or that is so obscure that they it may be completely new to them. It also means that they might be reading slightly above their age-level; a bookseller/librarian will be able to help you step the reading up a notch so you can challenge them without putting them off.

On the other hand, if the child isn't a reader at all you need to come at it with a different tactic. If they don't like reading, what do they like? There are books for basically every interest, and many children who don't like reading fiction will be able to while away hours with a fact book or a book about their favourite sport. If it's reading ability that is the issue, think about trying an intermediate novel (see Chapter 2) or something that is slightly younger but doesn't really look it.

What was the last thing they read?

Whether it was *War and Peace* or the back of a cereal box, having an idea of what they read last is a great starting point for picking their next book. Most people working in bookshops or libraries have a list tucked into the back of their minds called the 'if you like X you'll love Y list'. These are the go-to books that are always on hand to replace the really popular one they just finished with something they probably haven't heard of before. This list covers a large percentage of what parents come in looking for.

Books are a market just like any other, and when one thing succeeds competing publishers are ready to piggy-back on that success with plenty of their own offerings. Most children will be looking for something that will replicate the amazing thing they just read and so it is a great chance for lesser-known authors to get a piece of the pie. If you don't have a bookseller/librarian to hand, bookselling websites will often have a list of recommendations under their biggest-selling titles. This will help you when you're in a bookshop or library.

3 Bring them in

I know this isn't always possible, especially if you're trying to surprise them or if it's a gift for someone you don't know, but in many ways a child going into a bookshop to pick out their own book is a rite of passage. Kids get to a point where they want to start doing everything themselves and this is something you can do together with them taking the lead. Just point them at the right section and watch them go! All of the questions in point 2 above are more effective if you can ask the child directly and help them pick something that you can both be confident that they are going to love. However, if you're finding it hard to get them to admit what they want to read, especially as they start getting a bit older, this is the best time to get the bookseller/librarian involved.

Just a note: please don't be offended if we take the child out of earshot as we ask them questions about their reading habits. Sometimes kids get a bit embarrassed if they're still interested in books that might be aimed a bit younger, or if they want to start reading books that are a bit older and they're not ready to talk about it with a parent. This is completely normal and usually we'll find a moment to explain what book we're recommending so that you're still in the loop but the child feels like they've made a decision by themselves.

You might feel the urge to try to guide at this point, to get them to read to their age or to stay away from topics that are older. This is fair in some cases as you obviously have their best interests at heart, but do take a second to think: Is it time for them to make their own choices about what books they're reading? Are they old enough to know more about the world but you're just not ready to admit it? By pushing them to read more difficult books are you just making them feel as if reading for pleasure is essentially more homework? Taking a moment to ask yourself these questions might reveal more than you think. Allowing your child to make their own decision lets them know that you trust their judgement and sense of independence, which they will appreciate. This can be a great way to start developing your relationship into one where they are in the driver's seat, but they know that you will always be there to help if they need it.

4 Don't ignore the classics

One of the wonderful things about being a part of an industry whose shops and traditions go back for generations is that there are always so many stories from people who have been doing the job much longer than you have. One of my colleagues, whose mother owned the chain of bookshops we worked in, told me the story of how for years a sweet young boy would come into the shop and ask for 'Mrs Blyton'. He was convinced that the lovely lady who owned the shop had to be the famous author Enid Blyton whose books he always bought there. They had no idea why he thought this but no one rushed to correct him. Stories like this bring back a sense of the 'good old days', when kids didn't have their heads glued to screens and they stayed young long enough that they could genuinely believe that a world-famous author worked in their local bookshop and wrote the books just for them.

The 'classic' children's book is still a hugely valuable part of the overall picture and there is something lovely about giving a child a book that you adored growing up. The idea that you could be giving someone close to you the same wonderful experience you had when you first read it is one of the things we readers strive for when guiding the next generations. It's amazing to think that kids today are still reading some of the authors that our parents read when they were young, a lovely thread tying the generations together. However, we need to think about what place these books have in such a rapidly changing world. Between the language and the content of these older books, should we be encouraging them at all? There is a danger when we step back into the sensibilities of times gone past that we will remember that not everything was as rosy as we thought. Blyton's books have gone through quite a transformation since they were originally published. The American editions have been edited to replace character names like 'Fanny' and 'Dick' with 'Francis' and 'Richard'. Our own book market has been affected too, and any mention of the 'gollywogs', a toy family of black characters which are depicted with racially insensitive facial features, have completely disappeared from the Noddy books. Of course, Blyton isn't the only author to get this treatment and many books still have a lot of the 'old-fashioned' content in them. When I open the classic Peter Rabbit books I'm still shocked by how many times the adult animals beat the children with various things when they've done something wrong. Say what you want about the new film and TV adaptions of old books but at least you won't see a baby rabbit being beaten with a belt! (Although *Watership Down* still has something to answer for ...)

What can we do when these books are still around for our children to pick up? Should we discourage them from going near them? If we do that, we are simply making them more desirable. I think you should encourage them to read them, especially if they were ones that you enjoyed as a child. Sharing the joy of reading is one of the best connections you can make with a child.

A word of warning. Much in the same way that a lot of the language kids use now seems completely foreign, the 'classic' language used in older books might be a big challenge for your child. Make sure they understand that the book was written in another time and that the language was an attempt to help the children reading it to speak and act in a certain way. Although a lot of modern books have morals, they're nothing compared to the ones you find in older books. Once they get past the language barrier and read the book, then it's time to open a conversation. Ask them if there was anything in the book that seemed strange to them (besides the fact that children seemed to be able to disappear for huge stretches of time with nothing but a bag of jam sandwiches and some lemonade and their parents didn't seem to care) compared with the books they usually read. Through this dialogue you will be able to explain how the world and our perceptions of other people have changed. We shouldn't allow the legacy of these books to be completely destroyed just because times have changed. Allowing books to exist within context means that the kids of today will be better educated on how far we've come, and they'll be able to enjoy some amazing books that have been around longer than they have! Blyton was writing in post-war Britain and so was focused on creating an idyllic and safe version of the English countryside where children could wander and get into trouble which would be sorted by the time the book was over and they would be ready for another adventure straight away. Although they may have had to be adapted a little over the years for a new audience, the ideas behind the books are still relevant and create a very safe space for the reader, which is why they are so well suited to younger readers. Many people would like to see the books gone altogether, while others argue that the old books should be left as they are, relics of another time. I fall somewhere in the middle – let the publishers give them a new coat of paint to help them appeal to a new audience while also maintaining their original shine. When you take all of this into account when introducing the classics to children you will find that they can get so much more out of the book than they might out of a more modern title. I would also encourage you to check out any film tie-ins that may have been made since the book came out, as these can fill in any gaps left from the more challenging language, and watching the film is an activity you can do together to share your love of the story!

Reading by Stage

Pre-Natal Reading – How Young is Too Young?

In my opinion, there is no such thing as too young. Many studies have proven the benefits of pre-natal reading and it's a great excuse to read some lovely books.

During the last ten weeks of pregnancy, a baby can hear its mother's voice as it is amplified through her body. Because of this, maternal talking to babies *in utero* can help evolve their capacity for linguistic development later in life. However, we can go a step further than this. Studies conducted by renowned scientist Anthony DeCasper in the early 1980s presented proof that third-trimester foetuses could actually distinguish not only the mother's voice but also the book they were reading.

After birth, scientists used a technique known as 'high amplitude sucking' (HAS), where the baby was given a dummy that changed what they heard depending on how hard they sucked. Babies as young as three days old had already been proven responsive to this kind of testing and, because of this, scientists had a form of yes/no system where they could determine recognition and positive/negative reactions (beyond the crying we are all used to).

One of Dr DeCaspar's most famous experiments became known as 'The-Cat-In-The-Hat' study, where mothers were encouraged to read Dr Suess' famous book to their babies in utero. When tested using HAS after birth, the scientists concluded that not only did the babies respond better to the sound of the mother's voice, they also responded better to *The Cat in the Hat* than to other books, no matter who was reading them. On the other hand, some scientists, such as Penn State University's Dr Rick Gilmore, argue that while babies can come to recognise voices and the speech rhythms in their parents' voices, "nothing suggests that reading or the kind of material you read matters".

While this might be true and the real value is in the connection you're making with the baby, there is no doubt that reading to your bump can help you bond and get in loads of reading practice before the baby is born!

Books with sing-song and bouncing rhythms such as those written by Dr Suess are great fun to read, and the endorphins released while reading them are always a good side effect too. Having fun and strengthening your own relationship with books at the same time will help you and your baby through the whole process of developing a love of books. If you want to start making connections with your little one, something like this really highlights the amazing ability of reading to forge connections in ways that may otherwise be difficult. Just like any other form of art, books help us to express our emotions.

I would especially encourage this for parents who might not feel too confident with expressing emotions through words – let the books speak for you and take the awkwardness away. You might really surprise yourself. There are plenty of picture books that are able to make me tear up on a fragile day!

> **TIP:** Keep a log of the books you particularly enjoyed reading to your bump. Not only will it be a lovely reminder of your baby's first books but you can also try the experiment yourself and see if you get any big reactions.

Working the Market from the Beginning – James Joyce for Newborns

Imagine the scene ...

> The world as we know it is ending, lava is flowing down the streets, rain is falling upwards and the world's leaders are clueless about how to save humanity from certain destruction. Suddenly a message appears from the heavens; a series of letters and numbers so complex that even the greatest minds alive cannot decipher them. Is there any hope? Can humanity be saved? Then, just before all is lost, two figures appear. At first sight, it is an older woman and a small child but when you look closer, you see that it could be the answer to your prayers. You ask the old woman: 'Do you understand what the message is trying to tell us?' and there is hope in your heart as the woman smiles and pushes the child forward. It teeters, barely old enough to hold itself upright. 'But this is only a child; she can't be older than three!' 'Ah yes,' the woman nods her head knowingly. 'But she's an extremely advanced three-year-old.'

Dramatic as it may seem, in my experience hell hath no fury like a parent or grandparent who has been told that a book is too advanced for their child. I once tried to explain that *The Witches* by Roald Dahl was in fact, not suitable bedtime reading for a four-year-old who was still sleeping with a nightlight. As a woman in my mid-twenties, that book still gives me nightmares! It doesn't get much better when they're reading on their own. I'm no stranger to kids who are looking for a bit of a scare (*Goosebumps* are still constant sellers), but there is no way that you can tell me that your eight-year-old is ready for Stephen King's *IT* because he likes clowns and he half watched the old movie.

This chapter should help you to understand the importance of matching the correct type of book to the relevant age. Arming yourself with this knowledge will ensure you have all the tools you need to raise happy and confident readers for life.

So they're here ... now what?

Everything your baby is experiencing is brand-spanking new and books are the perfect way to take their new senses for a test drive. Here is where we put our knowledge of what books are on the market and how to use them to work.

Cuddly books for newborns

These do exactly what they say on the box. They usually have just a few pages and are made from soft (usually washable) material, which allows your little one to experience the design and texture up close. This is an expanding area of publishing and there are always new versions coming in to the shops. For very small babies, look out for either black and white or blocks of bright colour in the designs as these help to keep baby's attention as their vision develops.

After birth, babies' vision is limited to roughly the distance between them and their parents' faces when being held. By about eight weeks, they start to be able to see further away and learn how to focus. Using books at this stage is great because the high colour contrast helps them to focus with both eyes on the same thing. Added elements such as noisy 'crinkly' pages and plastic mirrors make these kinds of books the perfect distraction to bring in the buggy when you leave the house, as well as being a great way to help develop hand-eye coordination.

Picture books can also be great for this age but more for listening to your voice and seeing the colour. They're great for everything so long as you don't let the baby actually touch them...

> TIP: Don't forget buggy books! These are usually very small, simple board books with a handy tie that can be attached to the buggy. This really helps when your baby starts getting a laugh out of throwing things out of the pram!

Board books (2–3)

So your toddler likes to chew things ... and pull things ... and throw things? Then these are the books for you! Many of your favourite storybooks are available in this thick card format, so they're a great option when your little one is enjoying trying to destroy everything in sight.This sturdy book also allows for more intricate interactive elements such as lift-the-flap and pop-ups. Some of the newer generation board books also have light sensors for tiny hands and buttons for when they are a bit stronger. These books are usually a smaller size, which means that the little ones can start trying to hold the book themselves, allowing for an element of ownership and some imitation, as they have a book that is in proportion to themselves, just like you do. I find that many parents make the mistake of forgetting this stage and move on to paper books too early – while they are great for having bigger pictures, they only really work when the little ones can't get their hands on them.

You cannot blame babies for wanting to explore, and delicacy is not a skill they are born with! Tailor the books to their stage of life and your investment will reap rewards. The last thing you want is for books to be something they feel they have to be overly careful with, something 'grown-up' and not for them, which is not the aim here at all. We want them to see books as part of their everyday life – something that grows with them, not something to aim towards.

> **TIP:** Next time you are in the library or bookshop, make a point of letting your little one pick a book in the same way that you pick yours. Show your child that books are a personal thing as well as something you both share, and let them know that their opinions matter.

Picture books (3–5)

Does exactly what is says on the tin, doesn't it? It's a book with pictures … but why stop there? Without the lift-the-flap and other interactive elements, picture books start to rely more on actual plot as babies start to develop more of an attention span and are beginning to understand what you're talking about. Suddenly the books stop being something to rip or chew and instead start to become a route into their imaginations.

It is also at this stage that you start to get a fun thing called 'opinions'. Trying to win over another sensible adult is one thing, but it's a completely different game with little ones who have no concept of a reasonable debate! As such you might find that suddenly you can read nothing but dinosaur books or princess books or dolphin books, and any attempt to deviate from that results in tantrums, screaming and a not-so-pleasant experience in a place generally renowned for its peaceful atmosphere.

However, this is where you need to remember something: you are smarter than your small child! I know it might feel as if they have the upper hand in many situations, but you need to remember that they don't know everything! I have told numerous children over the years that we were closing the shop for the day at 9:30 am in an attempt to help the parents get them out so they could do the shopping! So use your bookseller to help you construct a narrative that will keep everyone happy. Need a book with a dog in it but you've read all the ones on the shelf? Did you know that a cow looks like a really big dog? We are there to help you and keep everyone happy, so let us help spin a few white lies ... publishing for children is so broad now that there are plenty of cross-over books with pirate princesses, and diggers that are also dinosaurs. There is life after reading the same book 1,384 times!

TIP: If you find your child is obsessed with a particular book, get a second copy. I know this sounds like a not-so-cunning sales technique on my part but, much like a beloved toy, books can hold a huge amount of comfort when children feel unsettled. If a copy gets lost or damaged beyond repair (it's amazing how many books end up in the toilet), you don't want to realise you don't have the special book when you're trying to get a screaming child to sleep.

Reading as routine

We all know how important routine is in our own lives. This is nothing compared to the importance of a child's routine in keeping them settled and helping their parents feel like they're in control at least some of the time!

Making sure that books are part of that routine comes with countless benefits: it can help settle them for bed and it's a relaxing activity you can do together, as well as helping them to associate reading with something fun and comforting, which will help to ensure they continue that positive relationship with learning as they grow. However, on a closer look, countless studies suggest that regularly reading to your children can have real and lasting effects on their ability to read and write, not to mention helping them to develop their ability to retain information, giving them a real head start for school and further education. The authors of *Handbook of the Economics of Education Vol. 1*, who include Nobel prize-winning economist James Heckman, suggest that throughout a child's development "skill begets skill", which means that, as children learn to do one thing, no matter how basic it seems, this can help them develop faster in another area. This building on their abilities stacks together building blocks to create a steady foundation for further learning as they progress into adulthood and beyond.

This theory can be found in many of the basic developmental milestones we see in small children, such as their ability to make nonsensical noises that develop into words and then into full sentences. From there they learn to associate those sounds with letters, then words and then sentences on the pages in front of them and then, suddenly, they're read-

ing! It seems like a simple progression, but once we acknowl-
edge the logic of it, we can start applying it to other areas, because anything we can do to help develop a child's basic skills
should be encouraged.

But how do we know that just reading to a child will really
help them as much as I'm claiming it will? A study conducted
by G. Kalb and J.C. van Ours of the University of Melbourne,
entitled *Reading to Young Children: A Head-Start in Life*, ex-
amined the effect of regular reading on over 4,000 children
from the ages of four to eleven.

They found "a direct causal effect from reading to children
at a young age and their future schooling outcomes regardless
of parental income, education level or cultural background".
The study focused on the effects of reading to a child every
day, which fits in very well if you can integrate a bedtime story into your child's night-time routine.

A customer put it very simply to me one day. Every night
they go through the three Bs: Bath, Book and Bed. It's as easy
as that! Finding that extra half hour in the evening to wind
down with a book is something that can be done by most and
can have real benefits. This is something that I'm particularity
passionate about because it doesn't need to cost the earth (or
anything at all if you go to the library). It encourages a stronger and more direct relationship between children and their
parents, especially as modern parents have to work long hours
and so may not see their children as much as previous generations of parents did. It has a direct benefit for the children
involved and can have lasting effects throughout their lives.

I hope this is particularly reassuring for parents who may
not come from a reading background themselves. I encounter
many parents who are worried that their own lack of education
might have a negative effect on their children's ability to learn,
as they don't feel that they know how best to support them

in meeting developmental goals. The anxiety that comes with doing as much as possible to make sure your child has more opportunities than you did is an everyday reality for many, so anything that can help relieve that is amazingly helpful.

As such, it's important to point out that the study cited above found that "education of the parent has no effect (or a small effect opposite to what is expected) on reading skill at age 4–5". In the time before children start school, the simple act of reading to them every day is doing more than you might think, without having to buy any specialised equipment or read complicated child development books to try and get ahead.

Building the framework for success at the same time as developing your relationship with your child is one of the best things you can do for them and yourself and, luckily, having fun reading together is something that does both.

So now you have some science to back you up, the hardest thing you're going to have to do is pick the right book – you're probably going to have to read some of them over and over again, so make sure you pick something you like!

The beginner reader: as easy as ABC

This is where it can get tough. As soon as kids start going to school, we have to relax the reins a bit when it comes to holding their hands through their book choices. Up to now, you have had control over what books come into the house and how much time is dedicated to reading them.

Now they are starting the amazing journey of learning to read themselves and, of course, this is not the time to let up. Shared reading time should still be an important part of your routine. Try to separate their relationship with reading from their relationship with school. You need to encourage their love of learning, but don't try to apply this to reading from the offset, as this will just lead to anxiety and a sense of school never ending. If they want to try reading themselves, encourage all attempts, but don't push it in their free time! Working together on their reading assignments at home is great and necessary, but don't shift their ideas of reading from pleasure to schoolwork or you risk tarnishing both.

When trying to balance what they are learning at school with what you are showing them at home it is important to know how they are learning so that you avoid mixing messages and making things confusing. If you can remember your own first reading experiences, you may recall that 'early readers' with basic words were not the most exciting reading. They served the purpose well and have lasted the ages with many people still coming into the bookshop looking for *Topsy and Tim* and then the Ladybird *Read it Yourself* books.

Most schools now teach reading through a phonics-based system (usually Jolly Phonics) which is centred on sounds rather than naming the letters. Children are taught forty-two letter sounds, which are a mix of alphabet sounds (one sound – one letter) and digraphs (one sound – two letters) so they learn to decode the words much more quickly than before. The sounds are put into different groups, which are covered one at a time, so when you buy for very early readers, you will find that the books are often separated into groups covering different sounds, such as 'Giraffe in a Bath' or 'Fat Cat on a Mat'. It can be useful to check their homework to see what group they are working on so you can match the readers to their reading stage.

TIP: Swap a phonic reader into your night-time reading routine without your child knowing. As already mentioned, kids learn all of their early skills through imitation, so hearing the stories that implement what they are learning is great for reinforcement. See what happens when you're reading the book and you pretend to get stuck on a word that they can now read themselves ... Let them help you and see their face light up!

From this point onwards, reading becomes more independent. Your involvement doesn't reduce but it changes. A new world has opened up in the form of books and literacy, but that doesn't mean they're ready for it all at once – you still need to be a curator up to a point.

Once they move on to completely independent reading, it's important to keep engaging with your child, and also, while taking a step back, to keep an eye on what they're picking up. Remember that the more freedom they have to experience new things, the more opportunities they are going to have to encounter new ideas. A lot of the time it will be completely out of your control. But that's okay!

When it comes to parenting, this is the first time you may have been able to take a breath and now you have to be able to trust that the foundations you have laid for your little one will help them through. You need to keep this in mind when it comes to their reading. As we discussed in the previous chapter, ensuring that our child is reading suitable material is important for a number of reasons: it helps supplement their school learning and it helps to make sure they're reaching their learning milestones. However, you may run into some issues of inappropriateness when you get to the stage where they can read on their own and are going to be able to find books in the library, at school or from friends.

As I mentioned before, early readers are the foundation stones of reading. Learning ABCs or phonics and building confidence is key so that they can start to read on their own. Thankfully, because at this point their reading ability is limited, it will be difficult for them to try to read things with inappropriate content. However, you'll be very surprised at how early they learn how to sound things out, so gone are the days of s-p-e-l-l-i- n-g things out so the kids don't know what's happening – be sure not to leave any literature lying around that they could try sounding out. The last thing you need is the little one learning a new word that they might not understand but that other adults might find a bit concerning if they go around shouting it!

You know what your child can handle at this age so use your common sense. Death and loss is rarely discussed in fiction for this age, and for some children, even the mention of a scary shadow can mean a few sleepless nights. Reading should be a way to relax and wind down in the evenings and a source of entertainment during the day, so if you can tailor your reading material to that you will save yourself a lot of hassle and energy. There's no harm in having a couple of books going at a time in order to separate the high-energy stories from the winddown variety to make sure they have the desired effect. You could even consider keeping night-time reading as a combined story-time for both of you, so you can still control what they encounter before trying to sleep and keep that reading tradition going for another while longer. It will also help them to separate the reading you do at home from their school reading. Although they may seem very similar, remember that what they do in school is for learning and what they do at home should be for relaxation and entertainment.

TIP: If you're afraid that they won't be able to follow two stories at once, don't worry. They can watch four different series on TV one after the other and follow them fine! If it is a problem, though, you can do a recap before starting again and see how much you both can remember. This has the added bonus of helping with their memory retention as well as having the potential for fun. Steal the idea from TV and do a 'Last time on ...' in a silly voice.

Joke books and non-conventional reading

We need to remember that the aim here is to foster a LOVE of reading and, just as with everything else, not everyone likes the same things. Reading different formats like magazines, joke books and other short format books still counts as reading, and even if they don't seem to be representative of the level your child should be at, you need to readjust your view. Kids learn how to read in school, and they often learn to love to read by themselves. No matter how that comes about, that is the thing you need to focus on. You might be driven demented listening to the same terrible jokes over and over again, but being able to just laugh and have fun with reading is what we're trying to achieve here. Use their interests to your advantage and chat to them about what they are reading and why they love it. Just because they are getting something out of it that you might not understand does not mean it is not valid. You'll build their reading confidence and will be in a better position to help them move on to something more advanced.

The idea behind reading as a hobby is that it should be something to be enjoyed. You might love the idea of your child being a complete bookworm, head stuck in a book instead of in front of a screen, but there are so many levels to love in reading that this single image isn't the complete picture. Books can be the portal into different worlds or they can give us a glimpse into our own minds. For some children they are something they dip in and out of as their minds flutter from one thing to the next, while others need to read a book cover to cover. Books let kids be someone else for a while, or a version of themselves that knows everything about animals, or that can make everyone laugh with a cheesy joke. The whole point is for them to see books everywhere and know they are always within reach, no matter what kind they want to read or how they want to read them. Just as not everyone's favourite food is the same, not everyone has the same idea of escapism. Just as with everything else, your child's choice should be respected – you can always have other options at the ready if they want to try them.

This is one of the times I really encourage parents to pick up the book their child is reading. This is especially important if you find you have misgivings about the level at which they are reading. Try to put yourself into their shoes and ask yourself what is it that they find so amazing about these books? Are they laugh-out-loud funny? Are they comforting and non-threatening? You might be surprised!

Middle grade (8–12)

The intermediate novel

So your little one has got through their ABCs and 123s? What's next? This is where things get even more interesting and it brings us on to a trend that has become more and more popular, what I like to call the 'intermediate novel'. Falling somewhere between a picture book and a prose novel, these books have become the natural next step. In these books the spaces between lines are bigger and, in some cases, illustrations are literally replacing words in sentences. Is this the start of a descent into the world of the emoji novel? Are we reverting to hieroglyphics? I don't think we need to worry about that! These books are simply the next stage of evolution for the developing reader, when children are gaining confidence and are ready to try a longer book, without the dreaded 'block of text' that is found in grown-up books. Some children will jump past this stage and move straight on to full-text books. That is very normal and might even be seen as the more traditional way to do things, as books where the words have joint billing with the illustrations are relatively new in their popularity. How a child will develop is generally down to confidence and comfort. This used to be the stage where we would have lost a lot of young readers. Apprehension at the idea of moving from picture books to 'text only' books could drain the fun out of reading as they struggle through too much too soon. Now, thanks to these intermediate novels, this is not so much the case, and kids can ease themselves into reading longer books. When it comes down to it, only two things matter here: Are the kids enjoying what they are reading, and are they getting any kind of value out of reading it?

Based on my own observations and those of the overall book market, children revel in these books. Here are characters they can relate to, lovable but a bit of a disaster at times, and hilarious, as in, 'laugh out loud because you may actually burst' kind of hilarious. They are exactly the kind of funny that most adults don't understand and that is just fine. Most of us went through the phase as children of trying to explain to an adult something we found funny and getting the smile of someone who is just trying to humour you but really doesn't get it.

However, I still encounter a lot of parents who are worried about their children staying at this stage for too long. And that's where we get to the more complicated idea of 'value'. This can mean so many different things – monetary, educational or personal – and they all apply here. Not all caregivers can afford a new book every few days to keep up with the demand when their child flies through them. It can be extremely frustrating when a new book in a series comes out only in hardback and your child demands it on release day. It's a difficult conflict – on the one hand you're excited that they're reading and have found a series they love, but on the other hand it can be hard to spend money on something with such a small pay-out. This is where rereading, book swaps and libraries come in. A child who loves a book will reread it. Favourite books become a comfort to them, a return to a world they are familiar with and that they know they love. These books are not part of the school curriculum. Recreational reading should be just that, fun and relaxing after a long day of school. At the end of the day, they are reading, and there must always be value in that. However, the way books are categorised is much more nuanced than the shelves on which they sit. The way we decide which books we buy goes beyond the industry standards, which are vital only to the organisation within the industry, not within your home. We must take what children love about these books and respect that, and in doing so let go of the notions of what we did or didn't read at that age and just let them learn themselves.

If we were to consider the idea that illustrated novels belong to a category of their own, we would be able to discuss how we can coax children to read other styles of literature as well, rather than belittling them and implying that they are dumbing down.

When left to their own devices, most children will move on as their understanding and curiosity grows; while we can facilitate that move, it is theirs to make and enjoy. Just because they still love books from another stage doesn't mean they won't grow to love and appreciate the ones that come after it, right up until adulthood.

> **TIP:** Bear in mind that although hardbacks are more expensive, they are also more hardwearing, so if you have a child who is prone to rereading, you might be better off investing in the sturdier edition. If a bookshop doesn't stock the hardback (in Ireland we tend to have a larger format paperback edition instead), check to see if they can order it.

Comic books and graphic novels

I think any children's bookseller would tell you that their top frustration when it comes to encouraging children to read is when the child is genuinely interested in a series or a book and the adult discounts it because it is a comic or a graphic novel. I know this is something that frustrates my friends who are comic book retailers, but it is different from a bookseller's perspective. When a parent and a child go into a comic book shop, they know what they are going to find. This experience is completely different from going into a bookshop where the child picks up a comic. Suddenly, having been told that they can choose a book they want, the one they want isn't good enough because it doesn't have paragraphs of words. I find that this usually happens more often to reluctant and dyslexic readers, who are often drawn to graphic novels precisely because they don't rely on blocks of text to tell a story.

You shouldn't assume that just because a book has pictures in it, it means that your child is getting less out of it. As the saying goes, a picture speaks a thousand words, and being able to connect the visual element of these books with the written part is just another form of reading and learning.

Deconstructing a picture requires analytical skill and helps to develop an eye for colour and design. You wouldn't discourage a child from going to an art gallery, so why would you try to stop them reading a graphic novel or illustrated book if it keeps them interested and happy?

You should also take into consideration how amazing the world building is in comics and how it can be hard to find the same experience in other media. There's a reason why there are so many superhero movies out now; the idea of a huge pantheon of characters who exist in their own books but also interact with others in the wider universe means that there is always more to read and learn in this modern mythology. Most children are sure to find at least one character to love and follow.

It may be frustrating to pay a lot of money for something that won't take your child very long to read, but you should try and consider the positive aspects. Check your library and second-hand shops and people selling their old comics online – there are so many ways to enjoy comics without breaking the bank. If you are in a position to do so, always check out your local comic book shop for advice and information on the latest releases. Not all comics are child-friendly and the covers can often be deceptive, so please go in and have a chat to find out what's best for your little one.

> TIP: If there is a particular superhero movie/ TV show that your child is interested in, use that as a starting point for their reading. Most comics have an extensive back catalogue just waiting to be found. This is also the perfect time to get to know your local comic book shop and the people in it. They will be invaluable in helping you to make the right choice and they can introduce your child to a new series.

Pre-teen and early teen (12–14)

When do I know they're ready for more adult themes?

The short answer is ... you don't, and you might never know. Just being around other kids means that as information is discovered about the world of grown-ups it is quickly presented to anyone within hearing distance whether they want to hear it or not. Of course, the information is being presented as fact when who knows where the original person heard it and how much it has changed as the Chinese Whispers made their rounds. And what happens then?

For most kids, the idea of going to a parent to question the facts can seem like the most embarrassing thing in the world. As they enter their teens, they're trying to figure out the world for themselves and it can seem like the world they occupy is completely different from the one their parents grew up in. Boys making crass jokes and girls talking about what they read about sex in a magazine becomes part of their normal interactions with their peers, so they assume it's not something that needs to be reported back when a parent asks how school was.

Of course there are exceptions to this. Many families have open conversations about sex and relationships and no one dies of embarrassment, but it can seem much easier just to cover the basics and leave out the finer details as you assume that they won't find out about those until later. The main issue with this is that they don't need to wait until they're older, they have the internet now.

With a few clicks and a private browser they have access to information they feel too embarrassed to go to anyone else about in person. However, the internet is hardly a bastion of truth and good intentions. If you feel a bit ill and Google your symptoms, you are presented with 'facts' from a million different sources, all claiming to be true. It's a cold, it's glandular fever, it's bronchitis or something much, much worse. If, as adults, we find it hard to discern the truth online, think about how hard it is for children who have no experience of adults lying or leaving out the facts.

So the question changes from, 'How do I know if they're ready?' to, 'How do I protect them when I know they're not ready?' This is where books come in! First of all, go to Chapter 5, where I have compiled a list of books that deal with sex and adult relationships in healthy and accessible ways. You then need to think about how you can equip them for whatever they might encounter outside the home. Here are a few tips for dealing with the internet before even broaching the subject:

1. Understand different kinds of websites
Not all sites are created equal. Anyone can buy a domain name and set up a website, but what you need to look out for is the suffix: .org is a registered organisation, .edu is educational. Anything else is unverified. By making sure your kids know the difference, they can already whittle down the amount of search results and they'll be able to tell at a glance if they can trust the source.

2. Leave a book in their room
If you don't feel comfortable going straight into the conversation, there are plenty of books that cover the basics. Ask if they would read a chapter at a time and then come to you

with any questions they might have. It means that they are learning about it themselves but they also know that you're there to help them if they need it. It is not a failing if your child doesn't want to have 'the talk' with you. Some people are naturally squeamish while others just can't think of anything worse than discussing intimate questions with a parent. The best thing you can do is give them information and the option to approach you, and then leave them to it. Unfortunately, kids often don't get to choose if they're ready to start growing up and now neither do their parents. This is a difficult and confusing time for everyone involved – your baby is growing up and the baby can't believe that the world is actually much bigger than they thought. By working through it together, using resources that are available everywhere, you might be surprised to find things that you didn't know everything either.

> TIP: Take a look at the other forms of media they are interested in. Are there TV shows they talk about or watch with friends? Think about the celebrities and influencers they might mention in passing. You might be surprised at how many of those things contain or discuss adult topics. You will get an insight into what they are being exposed to and realise that the 'grown-up' conversations might need to happen sooner than you had thought.

Introducing real life through non-fiction titles

One of the key points that I make to parents who are worried about introducing difficult topics to their children is that they are able to handle much more than you might think. Plenty of the classic books kids are encouraged to read have some fairly scary stuff in them! *Watership Down* and *Char-*

lotte's Web deal with death of friends and loved ones in a pretty no-holds-barred kind of way and *The Witches* and the *Goosebumps* series freaked me out more than I care to admit.

At least with these examples you could argue that they're fiction, so there's a degree of separation between the reader and the events that are happening to characters that have been made up. However, think back to your own childhood, when you were afraid of something completely irrational in the dark or you had read a book with characters that you really connected with; the last thing you were thinking was that they weren't real. The sign of a truly great story is that it feels deep enough to be rooted in the world around you, no matter how far from your 'real' world it may seem. So, whether the book is fact or fiction, you can believe that it seems pretty real for the reader if done correctly.

Nevertheless, it is true that the degree of separation that the page produces between terrible things that are happening in the book and the person reading it is a helpful tool for learning about the world around us. Sometimes it can be easier to process terrible things if they're presented in a narrative way where you can stop and take a break at the end of a chapter, as opposed to watching TV, where events are thrown at you as you sit passively in front of it. Of course there are teens who would prefer to strike out on their own and pick up something a bit more heavy duty. If that happens, do your research.

If you see them reading something that covers a topic that might be a bit heavier than they're used to, do a quick Google search to learn the basics of what they're reading about. In this case, knowledge is literally power, and the more you know about it, the better. If you're under pressure, bring up a Wikipedia article or a YouTube video that breaks it down into its most basic points. From there you will know if you need to be worried about the content and if you need to try to have a chat about the book. Don't automatically assume that they're going to be overwhelmed – everyone reacts to things in a different way. Just because a topic freaks you out, it doesn't mean it won't simply provoke a morbid curiosity in someone else.

One of the reasons non-fiction can be hard to gauge for young readers, especially teens, is that very little is published with them in mind. Beyond *The Diary of Anne Frank* and *I Am Malala*, both of which have been produced in editions for younger teens, it can be hard to know if what you're buying is going to be suitable. If a young child has an interest in a topic, you can usually take them to a well-stocked non-fiction section and find an illustrated book that deals with that topic. This becomes harder as their curiosity grows beyond the basic ideas and concepts. Be careful that they don't automatically turn to the internet when they start becoming interested in something; not everything on the web should be trusted. Literally anyone with an internet connection can make something up and publish it as fact. Instead, explain how to find reputable websites (see page 00), and get them to check their facts against other sites to see if they match up. Better yet, have them check it against a book!

If you find that the only books on the topic in question are aimed at adults, there are a few things you can do to make sure they're safe to give to your child:

1. Read it yourself

This obviously isn't always possible as it is time consuming. You don't want your teen to think that you're checking up on them or you could put them off the idea entirely! A quick flick through the table of contents to see if anything stands out to you is a good start.

2. Look up reviews

A simple web search of the book should bring up reader reviews that might give you an insight into the suitability and the accuracy of the book. It's also possible that the book in question isn't respected by the community specialising in the topic, in which case you might be better off looking somewhere else. You might get lucky and find a review by another parent.

3. Look up the author

It can be worth checking to see if the author is well respected online and if they seem to be uncontroversial or non-sensationalist in the way they express themselves. This is a great indicator of what a whole book written by them would be like.

Instead of trying to bring your teen around to what you're comfortable with, make sure they understand what they're reading and that they're comfortable with the ideas and how they relate to them. I'm not suggesting that nothing should be off limits (they are still very young), but there are age-appropriate ways of introducing them to tougher aspects of the world. They might even end up finding an area they're really passionate about.

The online worlds of fandom and fanfic

A large proportion of teen life happens online, so you will need to understand the intersection between reading and experiencing content online. Let's start with the basics: fandom. The *Oxford English Dictionary* defines it as:

> NOUN
> •1 mass noun: The state or condition of being a fan of someone or something.
> 'my 17 years of sports fandom'

> 1.1 count noun: The fans of a particular person, team, fictional series, etc. regarded collectively as a community or subculture.
> 'the Breaking Bad fandom'

For us, it's the second definition that matters. Being part of a 'fandom' allows fans of different series to find each other easily and share their thoughts. It's also a handy collective term when discussing the general consensus of the people within it. You will often hear people agreeing or disagreeing with 'the fandom' at large, or commenting that a particular fandom is 'weird' or 'strange'. All of this is subjective.

Fandom is a double-edged sword in many ways. On the one hand, it is great to have a place to go to share thoughts and feelings with people who understand. Growing up can be such a lonely place, so having the internet as a way to bridge the distance and find people who love the same things as you do is wonderful. On the other hand, as with most things, there are always those who will give it a bad name. Trolls and bullies can be found behind the keyboards here, so the same precautions should be used in all internet dealings, no matter how innocent a group may seem. You may feel as though your child is having particularly extreme feelings towards their chosen fandoms and there are a few ways to deal with this:

1. You're already starting by reading this chapter. Making the effort to understand what they're going through (no matter how cringy they find the fact that you're trying to talk about it) is a great step towards understanding your young person's feelings.

2. Remember how personal book characters felt to you as a child/young adult? Now imagine you had the ability to share your thoughts and feelings with thousands of other people. Can you blame them for getting a bit excited?

3. Getting lost in imaginary worlds is a great way to distract yourself from things that might not be quite so enjoyable in your own life. I'm not suggesting that everyone who has an intense relationship with the media they consume is having difficulties elsewhere, but it might be a good idea to sit down with them to make sure that they're not trying to get away from something in school or in their own heads.

4. If you're finding it difficult to comprehend the depth of feeling that your child is experiencing and think they should calm it down it a bit, please consider this: Would you tell a child who was really into a football team to 'calm down' about it? Of course you wouldn't, especially as there are usually plenty of grown adults who are showing the same emotions! The hysteria that surrounds sport and the actual tears that are often shed when they win something should be just as acceptable for people who are into things that just so happen to be more niche.

5. Look into it yourself. Try to understand what it is that draws people to it with such ferocity. Don't just assume that it's a 'kid's thing' and write it off. Media aimed at young people has to be more careful with how it discusses the world but it also has a licence to be much more expressive in its delivery. What you end up with is a form of media that is very entertaining, if a bit strange at times if you're not used to it!

6. If the themes and characters seem derisory and repetitive, please remember that they won't be to the young people reading about them for the first time. Please don't assume that all books that come out of a popular or topical genre are the same. When something becomes popular in commercial circles, it challenges authors to create books that tap into the trend while also delivering something new enough to hold the audience's attention. It is not an easy thing to do!

7. Finally, if you want to connect with your child over something that they seem to have very deep feelings for, respect them. You may not understand it, but they probably don't understand half the things you like and you expect them to accept those, so why should it be any different? Having an avenue for them to express their passion and creativity should be celebrated; you never know what opportunities might come from it. Most importantly, it is obviously something that makes your child happy, and who wouldn't want to nurture that?

YA (young adult)

Too much too soon? Introducing adult topics through YA literature

It would be easy to think that the YA, or 'young adult', category of books is relatively new. Many people can probably remember going from children's books directly into the adult sections. I'm sure most of us would agree that it did us no harm jumping straight into adult books in our late teens but, if you think about it, how many books did you read that actually starred and actively appealed to your age group?

If the answer is even one, then you've read YA literature. YA is not a genre like crime or sci-fi, but is part age categorisation, part warning. In my children's department the teen section has two distinct parts: the Teen section, which was for a reading and interest age of 12+; and the YA section, aimed at a similar reading age but with content aimed at the older reader. Teens can find books in the YA section that contain sex, drugs, relationships, violence and other topics that are beginning to become areas of interest as they get older. However, although huge numbers of teens find solace and excitement in these books, it doesn't mean the parents are particularly happy to see them on their shelves. I would often have parents come into the shop upset to have found their child reading a book with content they didn't think was suitable for their age.

If the child was twelve and they were reading a book with an age warning of 14+ then that would be one thing, but often it was the parents of 16+-year-olds who would complain. I completely understand the desire to protect young people from the more adult aspects of life – if you can keep them small for as long as possible, you feel that you can shelter them. That isn't always possible.

Access to the internet has given this generation an information overload, where all questions can be convincingly answered with a few clicks of a mouse, with no need for sources to be authenticated. Because of this, in many cases communication with parents has broken down. Why have an awkward discussion about difficult things when the answers can be found online? The generation gap is larger than ever and it would be tough to find a generation of young people who feel that their parents don't understand them quite as strongly as the current one.

In the past, bullies could be left at the school gate and sanctuary could be found at home but now, thanks to modern technology, it follows you everywhere, and there is little respite. To suggest that teenagers delete their Facebook or other social network accounts to make this stop is completely inconceivable to them, as their online lives are, to them, just as real as their physical ones. Turning their backs on their phones, tablets and computers would completely isolate them from their peers.

We are living in a country where abstinence-only sexual education is the only discussion some children are having with adults about safe sex, sexuality and peer pressure – having the conversation at home can be met with discomfort and rebellion. When you mix in the normal confusion and difficulties of being a teen, it is no wonder youth mental health services and the need for 'safe spaces' are in such demand.

Research gathered by the University of Arizona revealed that Ireland has the fourth-highest teen sexting rate in Europe, a very worrying statistic, not least because of how surprised we were to find out how high we ranked. Children as young as nine are sending sexually explicit material to each other, so to suggest that our young people are not ready to read stories about these issues is nothing short of delusional. If anything, we should be pushing these books into our children's hands, letting them know that what they are feeling is normal. Parents can use them as a resource to understand the pressure kids are under.

The wonderful thing about the books in question, and perhaps one of the reasons they are so popular, is because they do not speak down to their audiences and they do not presume to know more than them. They simply present scenarios which, even if they may seem fictitious to us, are the terrifying reality for so many young people.

Imagine living in a world where every embarrassing mistake you make could be recorded and held without your consent and then presented to the world at any moment. Where anyone sitting behind a computer can put on any face and present themselves as a friend only to betray your trust. On-line friends can share your hobbies and interests but these relationships are not seen as legitimate by others and are hindered by space and time zones. Thus they find themselves stuck in a contradiction; the ability to feel completely isolated in a world of connections. Having a range of books that speak to their unique perspective of the world is vital to helping them feel less alone.

> **TIP:** Books are the best conversation starters for kids and their adults. If you feel that your child is reading something that may be a bit old for them, instead of being a gatekeeper and stopping them (which will only make them more determined to read it), think about reading the book yourself, or even a review of it so you can anticipate some of the questions they may have. If it's something you don't know about yourself, think about doing some online research. As an adult, you should be able to find reliable information that you can then pass on, rather than leaving your teen to their own devices and coming across information that might not be correct.

Moving on to adult books

Through this whole process of raising a reader, the child in question has been your baby. They will always be your baby and nothing is going to change that, no matter how much they might try to fight it!

So when your baby suddenly wants to read the same books that you do, it can be a bit worrying. As adults we know how to process the pain, violence and complex emotions that are brought to life in adult literature, but how can you be sure that they're ready? YA literature is a great stepping stone, but although moving into the adult section will be an exciting step for them, it's quite a mentally difficult one for you.

As they've grown, you've been there to shelter them from standing directly in the blazing sun that is the real world. Making sure they've encountered things at the correct time and when they're ready is one of the big challenges of parenting; you want them to be as innocent as possible for as long as possible, but, unfortunately, they can't keep reading *Harry Potter* for ever, and sooner or later, in the same way that they started picking their own books when they were younger, they are now going to start picking things that even you don't want to read! So how can you get through the mental block of being okay with them reading about some dark things?

I usually like to say that teen and YA literature can be quite introspective; it's often about the main character and their personal experience of the world around them. Their perspective can often be quite limited, so that we can dive deep into the development of the character and see how they grow. It can usually be seen as a reflection of the readers' world too; the bubble of school life is quite small but is all consuming, and it can be hard to see anything outside of it. Even in the more serious teen books death rarely happens for no reason; there is usually a learning moment to be had by the main character that gives meaning to the horrible thing that has happened. This trend is changing slightly as teens are becoming more politically involved, but publishing is only just starting to catch up with that.

In adult books, however, it is often more about what is going on around the characters than about the characters themselves. Things happen in adult books and the characters have to work around the systems in place that are usually much bigger than they are. Because of this, the characters' experiences are felt more deeply and often need more room to explain and have the characters come to terms with them. Events are frequently random, as they are in real life, and often don't have a happy or even a satisfying answer. Adult book plots tend to have an added layer of complexity that the teen reader might find hard to engage with at the start, but if they're determined it won't hold them back!

You should also keep in mind that for many younger readers, a lot of the adult content may go over their heads, so there is no need to panic. Understanding usually comes in the form of knowing that there's something in the book they don't understand and so you need to make sure they know they can come to you with any questions they have. There is very little in the books that they shouldn't know about; all of it can be learned in a few afternoons in the school yard (usually in a less than correct manner), so why not take the opportunity to pre-empt it and make sure they're getting the right information? Keep in mind that there are plenty of books on covering adult topics with children. I discuss a number of them in Chapter 5.

> **TIP:** Start by sharing some of your favourite books that 'just so happen' not to have anything really adult in them! This way you can have a great discussion about the book when they've finished, as well as knowing that they're starting their journey into adult literature gently, and will know that not all adult books have to be about horrible things. You can also pick some books that you found an easy read so that they're not too put off by the jump in language.

Why Did They Stop Reading?

Trying to get kids to focus on one thing for more than two minutes can be a challenge at the best of times, so what happens when something that actually keeps them quiet for a while stops working? Just as you're feeling the relief of seeing your little angel sitting still and enjoying a book, suddenly there are half-read books littering the house and their enthusiasm for going to the library or the bookshop to pick out a new read has evaporated.

Well, first of all, it's nothing you did. Your ability to nurture a reader is in no way in question – this happens to almost everyone. Even as adults we can run into reading slumps where nothing is appealing and books you were excited about reading run out of steam after the first few chapters. You need to isolate the reason they've stopped reading and address it if it's something that needs to be worked through.

This topic can be broken down into the different reading stages, as the reasoning can be different depending on age and reading ability. If your child has additional needs or requires reading support, you won't find your answers here. Speak to your child's school or GP to see what changes can be made and what further action can be taken.

If it's the case that your child was previously enjoying the experience of reading and has now lost enthusiasm, read on.

Age 0–2

They're babies. If they're reading at this age perhaps you should let someone know? You could have a genius on your hands!

On a more serious note, make sure you're picking the right book for their stage of development so there is something that will catch their attention. Colour books will be lost on very tiny babies as they can't see much (see Chapter 2), and until they're two you might be better off with a book with interactive elements to help with their motor skills.

Other than that, maybe it's you who's losing interest because you're reading the same book too often and you're simply getting bored? If you are reading a book with words and a story in it at this stage, the story itself is going to be of more use to you than it is to them! Babies at this age will be more focused on hearing your voice and listening to its rhythm than they will be on trying to understand words they don't yet have the ability to decipher. The best advice I can give you is to treat yourself to a trip to the library or bookshop and pick a book that appeals to you so you can mix it up a bit!

Age 2–5

There are a few things you can do if kids are losing interest in bedtime stories and interacting with books in general. Think about your browsing habits. Are you picking the books or are they? By allowing them to make the decisions, children will develop a personal connection and the choosing process becomes a fun game you play together rather than one that has a winner or a loser. Of course, in the black-and-white world of a toddler you will still have to convince them against yet another book based on that really annoying TV show you hate, but try to reason it out. If it's based on an animal, can you play a game where you find another book with that animal on the cover? Or you could try to transfer the affection. Does the child have a stuffed version of the character? If so, then you can ask them to pick a book for teddy. They wouldn't want to read about themselves, would they? They already know everything! You might find that over time they will see that the characters in new books are funnier and more interesting than the media-endorsed ones.

Small kids are also very good at obsessing about one thing. Do your research before you go shopping or ask a bookseller/librarian. If it looks like they're not going to go for the usual topic ask them: What is the best thing they can think of in ten seconds? Get them excited about it and then when a book 'magically' appears on that topic it will feed into what is making them happy in the moment, not what made them happy yesterday.

Finding a book you like and trying to persuade them that they want it is usually a losing battle. Sometimes you need to remind yourself that you're smarter than them, even if it sometimes doesn't feel like it!

Age 5–7

This is the most sensitive age group to deal with because, in many cases, their enthusiasm for reading is directly linked to their confidence and their frustration if it isn't going right. Kids are like little pressure cookers; if they feel a slight frustration with something, they multiply it by a million. When I was small, I was literally reduced to tears when I was trying to do my spellings (who says cat doesn't start with F?), and I still remember the frustration of trying every variation of the spelling I could think of, only to be told I was wrong. When I was tested on it the next day, even though I had put in the work and had tried my hardest, I would still get in trouble for not working hard enough. That anger and confusion has stayed with me, and when I think of children working through the same thing with reading, I want to do everything possible to make it easier for them.

It's important not to mirror their frustration back at them. They're producing enough steam for all of you! Listen to them carefully and let them explain in their own words what they're experiencing when they're reading. Hopefully from there you can deduce if it's something practical like finding it hard to focus on the words, in which case you are better off talking to their teachers to see what help is available.

If it's the case that what they're trying to read is too old for them, then you could take a different approach to reading for pleasure. Make sure they can always return to a place of comfort with books at a level with which they are happy. School reading will be done and can be worked through, but if you force the issue in their free time in an attempt to get them through their difficulties quicker, you will make them resent reading even more. Imagine if you were learning a new system at work which was completely new and you were told to keep working on it when you got home instead of relaxing with something you want to do. It would hardly endear you towards it, would it?

If their reading is interest led, could it be that they're trying to read books which are too advanced for their reading level and that's what's causing the frustration? The book might be fine for them content-wise, but if the language is too sophisticated then any pleasure that can be gleaned will quickly be eradicated. Consider getting the book on audio and playing it in the car or before bed. Most new language is encountered in context and through conversation, so by listening to it, they get the part of the book they are interested in, which is the plot, without the thing that is holding them back, which is the language. Again, make sure what they're reading actually interests them. Do your research and ask around. This is a blossoming area, with publishers working to produce high quality but accessible writing with bright and fun illustrations.

Age 8–12

Once we start getting into the really independent reading age, the mystery of why kids stop reading becomes even more complex. It becomes less likely that the child has difficulty reading (of course this can still be the case and many children are diagnosed with some reading difficulties only at this stage), but because parents are not an active part of the reading experience for the most part, it is very common for them to lose track of their child's reading progress. Once children start getting that little bit older, they start to really form their own identities and begin to know their own minds. It becomes even more difficult to focus their minds and other activities start to take priority over something that requires them to sit still.

It is the parents of this age group who most often ask me what to do when their child has gone off reading. Sometimes you just have to come to terms with the fact that the idea of sitting down with a book is just not appealing to them anymore. Their schoolwork involves reading longer books, so they might feel that they're getting enough reading done in school and don't want it to be forced on them at home too. This is a good time to sit down and talk to them about how they're feeling and what really interests them. Then, much like when they were very small, you can start seeing if you can tailor some book choices to their interests, rather than forcing them to pick up something that has absolutely no interest for them.

The most common complaint I get is that kids are too into sport to pick up a book. Some people seem to think that those two activities are completely opposed to each other. I can understand it to a point, since one is quiet and solitary while the other is energetic and full of noise and teamwork. But that doesn't mean that kids have to choose which version of a ten-year-old they want to be. Nor does it mean that books aren't aimed at kids who are into sport. Children's publishing has seen a huge upsurge in sports fiction and non-fiction books. There is a great series of football biographies, shortened and written as novels for children, and so many kids who have turned away from reading flock into bookshops and libraries to get their hands on the stories of their favourite footballers.

So, when will they get the time to read? Trying to suggest to a child that they should take time out from their hobby in order to read a book, is a recipe for disaster. If they have found something that they love to do, either on their own or with their friends, trying to separate them from that for any reason is sure to fail from the start. Instead, you could re-institute bedtime reading for that wind-down time before sleep. With any luck they will have tired themselves out during the day, so the only thing they might be up to doing if it means the light doesn't have to go off is a bit of reading.

If you're finding it too difficult to drag them into a bookshop, having already had the conversation about their interests, find a book for them and bring it home. All going well, they'll see that you were listening and that you're supportive of their interests, and they'll have a book in their hands that allows them to engage with their passion even when they have to be in bed and can't be kicking a football or dancing around the living room!

The point here, as always, is that reading for pleasure is about absolutely nothing other than reading what you find pleasurable. That's all there is to it!

Age 12–14

At this age we can see many of the same issues. Pre-teens and teens have their passions and are very busy between school, friends and their hobbies. Add in social media, changing schools, exams, puberty and all that fun stuff, and you start to wonder how they find the time to sleep for half the day like little vampires. Fret not – there is still hope!

Most of it can be found either in reading about teenagers like themselves getting into bad situations or reading about

fantastical creatures completely unlike themselves. Seems easy? Like most things at this age, what they read is usually peer led. Of course there are still the devout readers who won't care about the reading preferences of the masses, but for the rest, not embarrassing themselves in front of their friends is the main priority. That doesn't really mean that they would be made fun of for reading, but dedicating their time to something that can't be shared in the moment might give rise to FOMO (fear of missing out), and that can put a lot of pressure on a teenager whose small community at school can feel like the whole world.

Sometimes a book comes along and grabs even the kids who don't read for pleasure. For my group of friends that was *Twilight*. I still remember getting the *KISS* magazine that had the first press photo from the movie – my friends and I were beside ourselves with excitement. It can be an amazing way to bring groups of young people together, but because book tastes are so personal, what you're reading can sometimes be hard to use as a talking point in a situation where everyone wants to fit in. So reading suddenly becomes something that is absolutely not what teens think is important and it goes by the wayside.

At this age, the worst thing you can do is force reading on them. When it comes to anything to do with teenagers, if they don't want to do it, you're going to have to come up with a really good reason why they should.

Look at other forms of media

This one takes a bit of effort and it may cause a great deal of confusion, but stay with me. Have a look at the TV shows and movies your teen is enjoying. If you can find something that was based on a book, fantastic. If this is the case, don't buy the book. This is a rookie mistake that will result in a book that remains unopened – why would they read something they've already seen? Instead, go to Google and speak to a bookseller. What books are people recommending off the back of the success of the show? You'll probably find a lot of 'if you like X, you'll love Y' books and it makes sense. If you love reading there's nothing worse than the book hangover, where you feel physically down because a book has affected you to the point of extreme emotion and has left you feeling empty now that it's over. It's the same with visual media. If you present your teen with a book that will fill that void, you stand some chance of them getting through it and maybe passing it on to their friends and reigniting their joy of reading.

You can use a similar idea with media that is not based on a book. A popular show is bound to have related publishing attached to it. This might be fiction (this goes for a lot of video games too – see Chapter 4) or non-fiction – fact books and the like. You will help them to gain access to some great reading material while showing them that you're listening and paying attention.

They might act as if it's super uncool for you to be showing an interest, but they will appreciate the fact that they're being noticed and also that they're getting some free stuff that's related to their interest. Try not to push the issue too much. If they read it, great. If not, it was an experiment that didn't work. If you try to force it or make a scene about it, you're just associating the experience with bad feelings and then no one wins.

You should also make a point of not judging what they're interested in. Some younger teens find comfort in things that are aimed at younger children but are still fun and can have a community element, like board games and collecting, while others try to seem older and get into darker phases. This is all normal, so just try to see it from their point of view.

Age 14+

When your kids pass fourteen, you need to start learning to trust them. If they're turning away from reading at this stage, you need to factor in everything that was an issue when they entered their teen years, then multiply it by 100.

At this stage they're trying to figure out what they might want to do with their lives after school, exams are getting harder and more important. Relationships are also getting more intense, with many teens starting to explore their sexual feelings. All of this really scary stuff is happening to them. More than ever they need your guidance but also your understanding. Now is a good time to have those conversations about what's going on in their lives and try to help them through it. See Chapter 5 for some guidance on how to broach a number of difficult subjects through books.

When it comes to reading for pleasure, make sure that they can see it as a great way to unwind when they're not studying and if they want to get away from social media for a while. You can also start talking to them about books you're reading and offering to let them have a go at them. Many older teens skip the YA section altogether and want to dive head first into adult books. Have a look online to make sure there isn't anything too horrible in a book if you haven't read it yourself, but give them the opportunity to start reading about some adult topics if you know they are presented and dealt with in a good way. That doesn't mean that only good things happen in the book, but rather that issues are covered in such a way that you can have a chat afterwards and see what they think. Or not; needless to say, sometimes the last thing they want is to discuss it with a parent, but at least you can rest in the knowledge that they're learning about some of these things in a controlled environment and not in front of a screen.

Reading-related disabilities

Some children, although they enjoyed being read to as very young children, never take to reading themselves because they have a reading-related disability such as dyslexia. People like to claim that difficulties such as dyslexia are more common now, but really it's just that we have the resources to diagnose and help those who have a condition that is actually fairly common. In generations past, many children were just assumed to be unfocused or unsuited to school, when in fact they might have had dyslexia. You should never think that bookshops and libraries aren't places for the dyslexic child. The people working there will be more than happy to help you find the perfect books. One of the best booksellers I've ever worked with is dyslexic himself and he can out-read us all any day!

So, what exactly is dyslexia?

How can such a small question hide such multitudes? The *Report of the Task Force on Dyslexia* (2001) suggests the following definition of dyslexia:

> Dyslexia is manifested in a continuum of specific learning difficulties related to the acquisition of basic skills in reading, spelling and/or writing, such difficulties being unexplained in relation to an individual's other abilities and educational experiences. Dyslexia can be described at the neurological, cognitive and behavioural levels. It is typically characterised by inefficient information processing, including difficulties in phonological processing, working memory, rapid naming and automaticity of basic skills. Difficulties in organization, sequencing and motor skills may also be present. (p.31)

However, if you ask anyone who has been through the diagnostic process and beyond you'll soon find out that definitions mean very little. They don't encompass the worry and heartache that can come with finding out that something you might take for granted, like reading, is going to be more difficult for your child.

One of the reasons I find this definition so helpful, however, is for one specific part: "such difficulties being unexplained in relation to an individual's other abilities and educational experiences". Dyslexia does not affect, nor is it related to, general intelligence. It does not mean there is anything wrong with your child's sight or ability to understand the content of what they're reading, it's just that their eyes (or ears as the case may be) aren't doing a great job at working together with their head to make things make sense. When you get into the science of it, there are many sub-sets of dyslexia with notable differences. Each of them can affect your child's ability to read and process information to varying degrees.

I am not a medical professional but I deal in the ways of practicality, and I know all too well that proactivity can be a great antidote to worry. If you find yourself at the receiving end of an assessment with the D word, here are some steps to help reassure you and your child that they do not have to give up their love of reading!

1. One of the main problems with the fonts used in most books is that they can be extremely confusing for the dyslexic mind. Consider the fact that the lower case 'd' is just a backwards 'b', and the same applies to 'p' and 'q'. The spacing between letters is very small and some typed letters, such as 'a' are not the same shape as you would typically write. These all come together to make the reading experience quite a laborious one.

   If you are a Kindle user, there is a dyslexia-friendly font available and you can change the size of the font on the screen to help too. For the physical book user, try to get books in the bigger 'trade paperback' size as the font will also be bigger.

2. Try to avoid books with funny fonts or that have words out of sequence or 'jumping' out of line. The only exception I will make to this rule, if your child wants to try them, are Liz Pichon's *Tom Gates* books, as they

have loads of illustrations and large spaces between the lines that help combat the kookiness!

3. Pay attention to the colour and thickness of the paper. Standard book paper is very thin and you will often get 'show-through', where you can see the letters printed on the other side of the page. This can make it difficult to focus on the letters you're trying to read. When it comes to the colour, the glare off the standard bright white page can also make it difficult to focus and can cause eye strain.

4. Pick books with illustrations as they break up the walls of text that can be quite intimidating. They also show kids that there are other ways of processing a story besides reading the words.

5. Finally, remember that all children come to reading at their own pace, whether they have a condition or not. With the right help, plenty of children with dyslexia come to adore books. Making sure they have the right tools to be given the best chance is the important thing here. (See Chapter 6 for more information.)

Ways to Foster a Love of Reading

Book clubs and other book-related events

As with any other hobby, sharing a love of books and reading is a great excuse to get together with like-minded people and maybe make some new friends along the way. This goes for all ages, not only the teens who have discovered the online world of fanfiction and fandoms! Of course, for the most part, reading is a solitary endeavour, but that doesn't mean everything around it has to be. Adult book clubs have gone through a renaissance thanks to the internet and the realisation that it's a great excuse to get together and share a glass (or bottle) of wine ... as well as getting to rant and rave about books that, up until that point, you may have felt completely alone in your feelings about! So, where to begin?

Baby book club

Becoming a parent, as well as it being one of the most amazing moments of your life, can be quite isolating. Between the hormones (if you're the one who gave birth to the baby), the lack of sleep (applies to all parents) and the effort required to find clothes that don't have sick on them, it is totally understandable that the idea of trying to get ready to go out of the house seems almost impossible. However, one of the best things you can do for yourself and your well-being is realise that you're not alone in what you're going through and that there are groups in your community you can join to meet other parents who are just as covered in vomit as you are, if not more so!

Baby book clubs are one of my favourite book groups because you never know what you're going to get! Some people come just to have a chat and meet other parents, others are excited to find some new activities they can share with their little ones and maybe try at home. Seeing your child interact with their little peers is always a joy as well as being important for their social development, which can help them when the time comes for them to go to crèche or school.

Baby book clubs are a great example of books bringing people together for reasons beyond just listening to the words on the page. You get to share a story and make connections with books but, needless to say, you get so much more!

> TIP: Check your local library and bookshop to see where the nearest baby book club is being held. If there isn't one, let them know that you would like to see one happening. You might be surprised how many people join in when you take the first step!

Book clubs for independent readers

There is a stereotype of the 'quiet bookish type' which starts when children begin to lose themselves into the world of books. People assume that they're not chatty or that they don't really have any interest in talking to people and would prefer the company of their books. This might be true in some cases, but for many children the reason why they don't talk much when they're absorbed in books is because there's no one around to talk to about them!

If you can imagine you loved baking but there was no one else around who liked cake, would you bother trying to share it? It's the same with reading. It's something that is done in isolation and can be enjoyed in complete silence, but it's even better when it can be shared with people who love it as much as you do!

When I ran a children's book club, I had a lot of children who were regulars in the shop but it was obvious that they were only there because their parents had dragged them along as a way to help them to be more social. Most of them were quiet for the first meeting or two, only really answering questions that were aimed directly at them. Then, as they realised that they had more to say than they thought and there were other people there who enjoyed the same books they did, suddenly there was no stopping them! Some children are naturally quiet and a bit shy, and we should never try to change them into something they're not, but so many of them, once they realised that they weren't on their own in the world of their books, found a voice and a connection with those around

them. Book clubs for children who have developed a love of reading outside the school system help them to develop their analytical and critical skills as well as their confidence in presentation and public speaking. Most of all, it gives them a social outlet where they can let their passion shine for a couple of hours a week and make some strong friendships through their love of reading. They are magical places!

Once again, check your local library or bookshop for book clubs in your area. If there are none, see if they would be interested in putting out a call for one. You could also have a chat with your child's teacher to establish if there are any other children who might be interested in forming a book club.

> **TIP:** Unless specifically asked not to, think about moving out of sight while the book club is in session. It might be tempting to hang around, making sure they're comfortable and having a good time, especially if they're shy, but it will make them feel more awkward if mum or dad is lurking in the background! They will tell you how it went, and if you have any concerns you can always take time to speak to the coordinator afterwards to see how they are fitting in.

Book clubs for teens/YA

The reasoning behind getting your teen involved in a book club is quite similar; it allows them to have another social outlet and it can have positive ramifications in other areas of their lives, especially the academic sphere. But as whole sections of this book attest to, the written word has a great way of broaching difficult topics in a way that is suitable for whatever stage the reader is at.

This is so much more prevalent in the teen years as they are encountering more and more adult content from their peers, the media and the internet. Joining a book club is a great outlet for teens – they can read books and discuss the themes shared in them in a way which is more relaxed than a school atmosphere while also being a safe space to share their thoughts outside of an academic setting.

One of the most eye-opening experiences I had when I was running a teen book club was when the TV adaption of the YA novel 13 *Reasons Why* started airing. There was advertising for it everywhere and there was a table in the shop with a generous pile of the TV tie-in edition of the book. The premise of the book is that a young woman dies by suicide and leaves a number of tapes behind addressed to different people, outlining why they were part of the reason why she decided to take her own life. Although we hadn't read the book for discussion, suddenly I had a group of young people in front of me asking why the TV show was creating so much controversy.

Here was a group of children who didn't feel comfortable asking their parents or teachers about something they had encountered but who were happy to ask someone they had known for a very short amount of time. I realised that this was a moment that was only made possible by the books around us and that we needed to have a real and honest discussion about what the book was trying to say, although the publicity connected with the TV show was trying to say something different.

I like to think that those teens came out of that meeting feeling that they had been heard and that they understood their concerns a bit better having discussed them. Books have the amazing ability to open our minds and make us consider life from a perspective we wouldn't have encountered otherwise. Having an outlet to discuss these ideas can be vital, especially for people who are at an age where they might be more susceptible to ideas that aren't healthy for them.

Book clubs provide just that.

> **TIP:** Keep an eye on what books are being recommended by the book club, not so that you can censor, but so that you can engage with your child after the meeting. Did discussing it with others change their mind about the book? Was there anything it in they didn't understand until they went to the meeting? It's a great way to open up a conversation and engage with them, so having a general sense of the book they're discussing is very helpful.

Technology

I know this might seem a contradiction, as we're constantly being told that we need to keep children away from screens. Yet here is a section dedicated to technology and how it can actually help children to love reading in every form. I think that's the most important thing – taking away screens is another conversation and one I am not qualified to lead. However, when it comes to stories, imagination and encouraging children to be involved, we should be leaning in to how they are engaging with the world, whether we agree with it or not.

Video games: the future of storytelling?

Of everything in this book, the opinion I express here could be one of the most controversial ... I think children should play more video games. I hope you will stick with me. I was a child in one of the golden ages of video games. The NES and SNES, the first PlayStation and the advent of the portable gaming console known as the Game Boy meant that we had a brand new way of spending our free time.

We talk a lot about today's children having so many different things vying to attract their attention, most of it summarised by the phrase 'looking at screens'. This evokes images of lethargic children with their necks cricked, bloodshot eyes just inches away from the screen. You imagine what they're looking at, basically just ads for violence and stealing, not to mention what's in the games themselves. I grew up with my peers bragging about playing *Grand Theft Auto* when they were twelve, and I was lucky to have been so innocent that I didn't understand half of what they were saying, but I knew it was stuff that I didn't need to be hearing about. Not to mention hearing on the news and in public discussion generally about how ultra-violent video games are causing a rise in violent behaviour.

The media does not present a good view of gaming as a hobby, but I believe that there is value to be found in video games as in any other art form, even at the same level as reading. I know this book is specifically about helping you to raise your child to be a reader and this may seem to be straying away from that, but I do think two of the most important skills you can teach a child are critical and artistic thinking, both of which can be gleaned from reading and, you guessed it, playing video games. Video games are another way for you to understand the world your child is living in and make a connection with them. I'm not saying they won't try to banish you from the room when they're playing, but taking an interest and striking up a conversation with them is never a bad idea.

So, how can we get value out of video games beyond them being a distraction? First of all, not everything a child does has to have educational value or be attached to a developmental stage, nor does it have to bring them anything other than joy. Many video games allow children to relax their minds and focus on something else after a long day of learning at school. Allowing your child to have enjoyable hobbies, even if you don't understand them yourself, is crucially important for the development of their sense of identity and independence.

How can you turn your child's obsession with video games into something productive? It already is productive! Imagine a book where you get to make all of the decisions and the action is played out in real time. You can stop and look around the amazing settings if you want; you're no longer restricted to the words on the page. In many cases, if you don't like the direction you're headed in, you can find something else to do and come back to the main storyline at another point. If things get too intense, you can go away and wait until you're stronger before dealing with it. You can invite your friends to join the adventure with you, as if they were reading the same book as you at exactly the same time.

That, in essence, is what modern gaming is all about. That is what you need to understand in order to make the connection with what your children are connecting with. Even games with mindless shooting now have a plot to go with them. Many are extremely perceptive about the modern world and use real-world logic. Shooter games are often set in real war zones, while sci-fi games often follow a strict set of rules.

There are even some games where the plot isn't action driven, but character driven, and you find yourself so attached to the people you are playing as that it can feel like you're mourning them when you finally put down the controller, much like you do when you finish a great book!

I'm not recommending that you should allow your child to play video games all the time. Looking at a monitor for too long causes eye strain and the behavioural issues that stem from any form of competitive activity should be kept in check. However, the world of video games is not restricted to teenage boys in dark bedrooms never coming into the light. They have become a genre-based media, and games for all tastes are being released.

Writing for video games is just as legitimate a form of artistic expression as any other writing and it's certainly a much more sociable one. From development to actually playing the game, gaming is a team effort.

So, if you find you have a child who seems to be stuck in an online world, don't assume that they are too far away to be connected with. Sometimes you just need to make the effort to go to them. You never know, you might find you like it!

Look into books in the same genre as the games they like to play. If you have someone who is obsessed with *Call of Duty* and shooting games, try some historical war fiction or books that are set in modern war zones (Andy McNab has an amazing series along these lines). The same goes for sci-fi and fantasy – find what your kid is attracted to in the games and work with it!

> TIP: Video games are a great gateway into books too. Most of the biggest game series have novelisations that follow the original plot, as well as having what is called an 'expanded universe' with the back stories and dedicated series for different characters that may not have had much screen time or

> development in the game itself. Video games, in
> their pursuit of the ultimate interactive experience,
> can sometimes lack the time and scope to flesh
> out the world around the plot. That is where the
> books come in. The amazing scenes that are shown
> in these games can be reproduced through the
> written word with a much smaller budget, so you
> get a lot more story for far less investment.

E-books versus physical books

Back in 1971, a student called Michael Hart decided to use the time he had on a giant Xerox mainframe computer in the materials research lab of the University of Illinois to start a radical new project. He transcribed the American Declaration of Independence onto 'ARPAnet', which would later become the internet we all know and love. He then did something unheard of and made it available to download. Only six people did so, but in that moment Michael created the first e-book, a step in technology that would reverberate throughout the book industry until it became the format giant it is today.

Although the press speculated that the e-book, with its convenience and lower price point, would eventually kill the print book, e-book and e-reader sales have now plateaued and the print book is making a good comeback.

What is the best way for your child to read a book? I would say that it doesn't matter how they read the books just so long as they're reading. However, the question is so much bigger than that and we need to consider the merits of both. I've seen plenty of passionate debates arguing both sides but here I want to make arguments for both!

- **E-books**

As a modern solution to a modern problem, it could be argued that e-books are better for the environment as they do not require the paper and other printing resources for each copy to be created. The effort and resources it took to create the reader itself are all that's needed to allow you to enjoy as many books as the reader can hold. Taking into consideration the air miles it takes to get a book to you and the resources it took to produce it in the first place, you can see how using an e-reader is the more eco-friendly option.

Of course, there is also the price element. Not everyone has the luxury of making reading for pleasure a priority in their children's lives and so if, for the one-time expense of an e-reader, their child can have the books they want for sometimes ten per cent of the price of the print edition that can be extremely appealing. You can also get apps to read the books on your phone so the one-time cost of an e-reader can be mitigated.

E-readers have the added benefit of often being more accessible to people with different needs than print books. Libraries are often the only places you can get books with larger print for those who are visually impaired; their range is usually limited as they are very costly to print and not widely used. With an e-reader you have the choice of font size as well as back-lit options to make the reading experience easier.

E-readers are extremely portable and are very handy when you are on holiday and are planning on reading as much as possible. Trying to fit seven paperbacks into your luggage at the expense of clothes is not fun! It also means that if you don't like the book you're reading, you can just download another one instead of being stuck with the ones you have on hand, especially if you're in a foreign country and none of the available books are in your language!

> TIP: Always make sure you're downloading the official version of a book to your e-reader. Although pirated versions are often much cheaper, they're illegal, and are often littered with errors and misspellings.

- **Physical books**

In so many ways, nothing beats a physical book. The ability to collect and add to your shelves is something that just can't be done with an e-book. Having your shelves as a conversation point in your home is an amazing way to connect with people, and allowing them to borrow a book is both an act of faith and a great gift. Because of licensing you can't lend an e-book to your friends. It is also very hard to get an author to sign an e-book and even if you could, I don't think it would be as special!

You should also consider what the super-low pricing of e-books is doing to the market overall. Think of how many people put a huge amount of work into each book and then ask yourself how much of that 99 cents they are going to see. Books are a valuable commodity and should be respected as such. In addition, if the manufacturer of an e-reader stops supporting a particular model to focus on a new, more expensive one, you will end up being left behind. You should also consider that if the e-reader manufacturer goes out of business, you do not physically own the books you have bought. You need the e-reader and their technology to read them. If the manufacturer disappears, you are left with nothing!

The satisfaction of seeing how far you've read and being able physically to flick back to parts you want to revisit is something you just can't replicate with a percentage in the corner of a screen. There are some kinds of books, reference books in particular, which just don't lend themselves to the e-book format, as you need to be able to jump from page to page with ease. E-books are not childproof and, like other forms of technology, are easily broken by clumsy hands. Physical books can be destroyed too, but if they rip one up it isn't going to hinder their ability to read all of the others that are available to them.

It is also extremely important that children have some creative outlets that aren't centred on a computer screen. Although the size and general shape of e-books and physical books may be similar, children need to know that they have an alternative when they're told to do something other than look at a screen.

Whatever way you or your child reads, the most important thing is that you are both enjoying it. We need to support the industry in whatever way we can, be it going to book events in our areas or making sure to support our local bookshops and libraries. Just because you have an e-reader, that doesn't mean you don't ever buy physical books and vice versa.

Books that Deal with Difficult Issues

This chapter comes with a warning. I am not a child psychologist, nor am I qualified to tell you how to deal with stressful emotional situations beyond my own experiences. What I can do is present you with books that I hope will help you start conversations with your children about things they might be going through. Because different stages of their development call for different ways of presenting information, I've broken each topic into age ranges so that you can pick the books that are right for your child.

Please be aware that especially for teen/YA, the difference in content can be quite big; just because a child is reading ahead of their age, that doesn't mean that they're ready for the older books, as this is where the difference really becomes apparent.

You should never be ashamed of using a book to try to get your point across when you feel that you don't have the words to articulate it yourself. Many of these issues may be things that you've experienced in your own life and you're not ready to have the full conversation as it can be extremely taxing emotionally. Children's books have the amazing ability to break even the most complex ideas into parts that can be understood by the littlest of people, so they might help you to understand things better too. The whole point of literature is to translate the human experience into the written word. Use that to your advantage and the books can become building blocks to starting your own conversation and easing some of the pain you might be feeling. Children are intuitive and notice even the smallest changes in people, so sometimes getting on their level and explaining the world around them is the best thing to do, even if the thought of it can be a bit intimidating.

Bereavement

This topic, maybe more than any other, is one where the style in which the information is delivered is extremely age specific. When it comes to grief there is a lot of cross-over; there isn't a one-size-fits-all. You might find, that for very young children, a story about an animal who is going through what your little one might be feeling is a good way to introduce a degree of separation so that they don't feel the book is too intense or sad. Stories such as these help you to start talking about how the other bereaved animals are feeling and why.

When kids get older, having a book that deals with the issue in such an obvious way can seem patronising to some, but others will feel that someone understands what they are going through. You might find that there is very little point in beating around the bush as they get older, and you are more likely to get more honest answers out of them about how they're feeling if you're honest with them and speak to them like the little adults they are.

The hardest part is that it is more than likely that you are also experiencing some extreme emotions and it can feel overwhelming to have to try and help a child process grief at the same time. That's why a book that will help you take some of the first steps can be so useful. Every child is different and finding what works for you and for them is the most important thing.

Picture books (3–7)

The Memory Tree
Britta Teckentrup
Orchard Books

Fox has lived a long and happy life in the forest, but now he is tired. He lies down in his favourite clearing and falls asleep forever. Before long, Fox's friends begin to gather in the clearing. One by one, they tell stories of the special moments they shared with Fox. As they share their memories, a tree begins to grow, becoming bigger and stronger with each memory, sheltering and protecting all the animals in the forest, just as Fox did when he was alive.

I think this book is perfect for all ages. It's straight to the point while also being gentle and kind. It reminds us that when a person leaves us, they are still in our hearts and that we should remember the joy they brought as well as being sad that they are gone.

Badger's Parting Gifts
Susan Varley
Andersen Press

Badger is so old that he knows he must soon die, so he does his best to prepare his friends. When he finally passes away, they are grief-stricken, but one by one they remember the special things he taught them during his life. By sharing their memories, they realise that although Badger is no longer with them physically, he lives on through his friends.

If you prefer to use the term 'dying' rather than just 'falling asleep', this book is a little bit more realistic, but still has the same message of remembrance and joy.

Independent reader (7–11)

Gangsta Granny
David Walliams
Illustrated by Tony Ross
HarperCollins Children's Books

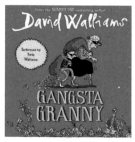

Our hero, Ben, is bored beyond belief when he is made to stay at his grandma's house. She's the boringest grandma ever: all she wants to do is to play Scrabble and eat cabbage soup. But there are two things Ben doesn't know about his grandma: One, she was once an international jewel thief; Two, all her life, she has been plotting to steal the Crown Jewels, and now she needs Ben's help ...

David Walliams is the current king of kids' books and for good reason. His books are hilarious and really speak to children at their level. He is also great at dealing with real-life situations and this book is no different. Granny passes away at the end, which is very sad, but the point of the book is the adventures she had throughout her life and the relationship she builds with her grandson, which is the most important thing!

Time Travelling with a Hamster
Ross Welford
HarperCollins Children's Books

On Al Chaudhury's twelfth birthday his beloved Grandpa Byron gives him a letter from Al's late father. In it Al receives a mission: to travel back to 1984 in a secret time machine and save his father's life.

Al soon discovers that time travel requires daring and imagination. It also requires lies, theft, setting his school on fire and ignoring philosophical advice from Grandpa Byron. All without losing his pet hamster, Alan Shearer...

A brilliant adventure with themes of loss and bereavement at its core. The main character's father dies before the book starts but the lasting feelings of loss are dealt with brilliantly. Ross Welford has an amazing way with words and this book is perfect for the more astute reader who may be finding it hard to express emotions around loss.

Teen (12–14)

Bridge to Terabithia
Katherine Paterson
HarperCollins Children's Books

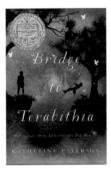

Jess Aarons has been practising all summer so he can be the fastest runner in the fifth grade. And he almost is, until the new girl in school, Leslie Burke, outpaces him. The two become fast friends and spend most days in the woods behind Leslie's house, where they invent an enchanted land called Terabithia. One morning, Leslie goes to Terabithia without Jess and a tragedy occurs. It will take the love of his family and the strength that Leslie has given him for Jess to be able to deal with his grief.

The death of a friend is something that will be extremely difficult for a child to process and this book understands that and is not preachy in its delivery. Jess is given room to process his loss in his own way. It is a devastating book about a devastating situation and I would recommend that parents read it too to help them to understand what their child is going through.

The Thing About Jellyfish
Ali Benjamin
Macmillan Children's Books

Everyone says that it was an accident ... that sometimes things 'just happen'. But Suzy won't believe it. Ever. After her best friend dies in a drowning accident, Suzy is convinced that the true cause of the tragedy was a rare jellyfish sting. Retreating into the silent world of her imagination, she crafts a plan to prove her theory – even if it means travelling the globe, alone. Suzy's achingly heartfelt journey explores life, death, the astonishing wonder of the universe ... and the potential for love and hope right next door.

One for the older teen, this book takes the reader through all the stages of a teen's grief, including outright denial. Although slightly fantastical, Suzy's journey is a real insight into a teen's mind.

YA (14+)

A Monster Calls
Patrick Ness
Walker Books

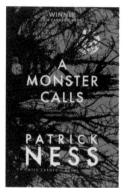

Conor has the same dream every night, ever since his mother first fell ill, ever since she started the treatments that don't quite seem to be working. But tonight is different. Tonight, when he wakes, there's a visitor at his window. The visitor is ancient, elemental, a force of nature, and wants the most dangerous thing of all from Conor. It wants the truth.

This book is heartbreaking but very real. The manifestation of Conor's grief destroying everything around him is as close to a child's real feelings as you might get.

The Book Thief
Markus Zusak
Black Swan

1939. Nazi Germany. The country is holding its breath. Death has never been busier. Liesel, a nine-year-old girl, is living with a foster family on Himmel Street. Her parents have been taken away to a concentration camp. Liesel steals books. This is her story and the story of the inhabitants of her street when the bombs begin to fall.

This book is a classic for a reason. Narrated by Death himself, there is an element of separation from the main character which allows us to see loss from every angle and the journey people go through to process it.

LGBT Relationships

This can be a very difficult area to broach with your children for many reasons. It is also important to explain that different sexualities are just part of everyday life. As children get older you can start introducing books about people questioning their sexuality and learning about themselves so that they can feel free not only to be themselves but also to have empathy for those around them.

Discussions on gender identity and sexuality are becoming more and more mainstream and while you may find it a tough topic, odds are that your teens and young adults are already having those chats with their peers. This section, maybe more than any other, is one that I would encourage you to have a look through so that you might see these ideas through their eyes. We grew up in generations where our sexualities were very private and we were encouraged to be that way. Now young people are not afraid to be out and proud, and though they may still face many obstacles, they are facing them with optimism and hope, something that is very much reflected in these books.

Picture books (3–7)

It's Okay to Be Different
Todd Parr
Little, Brown and Company

It's okay to need some help. It's okay to be a different colour. It's okay to talk about your feelings. It's okay to make a wish ...

This book is more of a conversation starter than specifically about relationships, but by reading this to your child you can always refer back to it when they encounter something they don't understand.

Introducing Teddy
Jessica Walton
Illustrated by Dougal MacPherson
Bloomsbury Children's Books

Errol and his teddy, Thomas, are best friends who do everything together. Then Thomas the Teddy finally tells Errol what Teddy has been afraid to say: 'In my heart, I've always known that I'm a girl teddy, not a boy teddy. I wish my name was Tilly.' And Errol says, 'I don't care if you're a girl teddy or a boy teddy! What matters is that you are my friend.'

This extremely sweet picture book is the perfect way to explain trans identities to little ones. It shows that by accepting who Tilly is, everything in Errol's relationship with her stays the same, except now his best friend gets to be herself and even happier!

Independent reader (7–11)

George
Alex Gino
Scholastic

When people look at George, they think they see a boy. But she knows she's not a boy. She knows she's a girl. George thinks she'll have to keep this a secret forever. Then her teacher announces that their class play is going to be *Charlotte's Web*. George really, really, REALLY wants to play Charlotte. But the teacher says she can't even try out for the part, because she's a boy.

This is another book I would recommend that everyone read. It offers a real perspective of someone growing up as a transgender person and has empathy and hope at its core.

Teen (12–14)

Yay! You're Gay! Now What?
Riyadh Khalaf
Frances Lincoln Children's Books

In this personal, heartfelt go-to guide for young queer guys, YouTuber and presenter Riyadh Khalaf shares frank advice about everything from coming out to relationships, as well as interviews with inspirational queer role models, and encouragement for times when you're feeling low.

Free To Be Me
Dom&Ink
Penguin

Queer people have so many amazing role models to look up to. This book frames coming out as something that should be celebrated, even if it isn't always easy. Every rainbow-coloured page is packed with LGBTQ+ activities, advice and attitude. Read quotes from real-life rainbow icons, find out how to throw your own Pride Party, and learn about the history of gay rights. Most importantly: celebrate being yourself and what makes YOU amazing!

This book is ideal for any young person who is trying to navigate the minefield that is figuring out their identity. Another wonderfully positive book, this one applies to every colour in the rainbow and focuses on inner acceptance as well as the community waiting for them!

YA (14+)

This Book is Gay
Juno Dawson
Illustrated by Spike Gerrell
Hot Key Books

A funny and pertinent book about being lesbian, bisexual, gay, queer, transgender or just curious – for everybody, no matter their gender or sexuality.

This is very much for young adults. Imagine it as a sexed book for queer kids and then some! Everything in this book can be found online, but having a resource from a trusted source is always the safer bet. If you pick it up yourself, you'll be sure to learn a lot.

Proud: Stories, Poetry and Art on the Theme of Pride
Juno Dawson (compiler)
Stripes Publishing

A stirring, bold and moving anthology of stories and poetry by top LGBTQ+ YA authors and new talent, giving their unique responses to the broad theme of pride. A celebration of LGBTQ+ talent, *Proud* is a thought-provoking, funny, emotional read.

This is a fantastic anthology and a great read as well as being extremely empowering. It's also a great way to find some new authors to move on to if you like the style of their short stories.

Queen of Coin and Whispers
Helen Corcoran
The O'Brien Press

This fantasy novel has political intrigue and adventure at every turn, and is a truly wonderful example of having an LGBTQ+ relationship at the front and centre for no other reason than the fact that the main characters happen to be gay.

This is the quintessential example of a book that is representative and diverse but is also an amazing story, creating a world that normalises characters with different experiences and orientations.

Cover image courtesy of The O'Brien Press Ltd

Race

I wanted to bring together a list of books representing many different experiences from across the world. My book will mostly be bought and read in Ireland in predominantly white contexts, so this section presents books that show children from different racial and cultural backgrounds. Publishers are really coming to terms with the fact that it is not only white, middle-class people who read their books and that everyone deserves to be represented in what they see on the bookshelves.

Many of these books do not feature race or religion as the sole plot of the story, rather they feature children of different races and religions. Allowing children to broaden their understanding of the world and the people in it by reading widely is one of the greatest gifts you can give them. It promotes tolerance and empathy and means that children can focus on what makes them the same as others while also celebrating what makes us different. The world around us is so varied and interesting, and children deserve to see and experience it!

Picture books (3–7)

Elmer
David McKee
Andersen Press

Elmer is different. Elmer is patchwork. The grey elephants all love him, but he soon starts to wonder what it would be like to be just the same as them ...

Full of colour, wisdom and pathos, little readers will love this classic tale at bedtime. A quintessential book of being different and being celebrated for it, *Elmer* brings its core message to children in a bright and cheerful way!

Sulwe
Lupita Nyong'o
Illustrated by Vashti Harrison
Penguin Books

Sulwe's skin is the colour of midnight. She's darker than everyone in her family, and everyone at school. All she wants is to be beautiful and bright, like her mother and sister. Then a magical journey through the night sky opens her eyes and changes everything.

This is one of the most beautiful and heart-wrenching picture books I've ever encountered. It mixes mythology with an amazing story of self-love, based on Lupita Nyong'o's own childhood experiences.

Little People Big Dreams: Rosa Parks
Lisbeth Kaiser
Illustrated by Marta Antelo
Frances Lincoln Publishers

Rosa Parks grew up in Alabama, where she learned to stand up for herself at an early age. Rosa went on to become a civil rights activist. In 1955, she refused to give up her seat to a white man on a segregated bus, sparking the

Montgomery Bus Boycott. Her courageous decision had a huge impact on civil rights, eventually leading to the end of segregation on public transport.

This book is one of the *Little People, Big Dreams* series, which is the perfect way to introduce small children to the amazing people who have paved the way for human rights throughout history. They present the facts in extremely child-friendly ways and are sure to have children engaged and asking loads of questions!

Independent reader (7–11)

Little Badman and the Invasion of the Killer Aunties
Humza Arshad & Henry White
Illustrated by Aleksei Bitskoff
Penguin Books

"You've probably heard of me, right? Little Badman. No? Oh. Well ... Doesn't matter. You will do one day. I'm gonna be big.

"I'm Humza Khan, the greatest eleven-year-old rapper Eggington has ever known; soon everyone will know my name."

Comedian Humza Arshad has taken the UK children's market by storm with this hilarious new series. It also gives great insight into the Muslim community in the UK.

Kick
Mitch Johnson
Usborne Publishing

Budi's plan is simple. He's going to be a star. He's going to play for the greatest team on earth, instead of sweating over each stitch he sews, each football boot he makes. But one unlucky kick brings Budi's world crashing down. Now he owes the Dragon, the most dangerous man in Jakarta. Soon it isn't only Budi's dreams that are at stake, but his life.

By describing the struggles of the Indonesian workers using something to which children can relate, like football, *Kick* shows children that not everyone's childhood is the same and that we need to work together to bring everyone up.

Teen (12–14)

The Weight of Water
Sarah Crossan
Bloomsbury Publishing

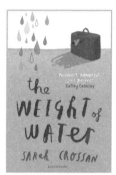

Armed with a suitcase and an old laundry bag filled with clothes, Kasienka and her mother head for England. Life is lonely for Kasienka. At home her mother's heart is breaking and at school friends are scarce. But when someone special swims into her life, Kasienka learns that there might be more than one way for her to stay afloat.

Sarah Crossan is the queen of the verse novel and this book is the proof of that. As well as being the ideal read for teens who may not have a long attention span for books, this amazing book also manages to encapsulate the feelings and experiences of a child moving to a new country and trying to learn the language and fit in. It is a must-read for teens and adults.

YA (14+)

The Hate U Give
Angie Thomas
Walker Books

Sixteen-year-old Starr lives in two worlds: the poor neighbourhood where she was born and raised, and her posh high school in the suburbs. The uneasy balance between them is shattered when Starr is the only witness to the fatal shooting of her unarmed best friend, Khalil, by a police officer. Now what Starr says could destroy her community. It could also get her killed.

This book changed the world when it was first released a few years ago. In a time of extreme racism and racial tension, it showed that behind the headlines there were people whose voices were struggling to be heard. *The Hate U Give* started a trend of activism through teen literature that has yet to slow down.

When Dimple Met Rishi
Sandhya Menon
Hodder & Stoughton

Meet Dimple. Her main aim in life is to escape her traditional parents, get to university and begin her plan for tech world domination.

Meet Rishi. He's rich, good-looking and a hopeless romantic. His parents think Dimple is the perfect match for him, but she's got other plans ...

Dimple and Rishi may think they have each other figured out. But when opposites clash, love works even harder to prove itself in the most unexpected ways.

This rom-com has all of the heart and sweetness you could want from the best summer reads, but it is also hard-hitting and real.

Body Image

Our relationships with our bodies range from love to hate and everything in between depending on the day of the week. As we have grown, society has told us what shape we should be and many of us tie ourselves in knots trying to achieve it. Helping your children develop a healthy relationship with their bodies, no matter what their shape, is an extremely important and often difficult task. Children learn their early opinions and habits from their parents and the adults close to them, so making sure they're able to love what their body can do is vital!

Teens are constantly bombarded with images and often have body-shame pushed on them by their peers as well as by society. Many of us have experienced the struggle that comes with trying to look the way we think we need to look in order to be happy. By letting your kids know that there are so many ways to be happy with the way they look, you allow them to put that brainpower to use somewhere else.

Picture books (3–7)

Minnie & Max are OK!
Chris Calland and Nicky Hutchinson
Illustrated by Emmi Smid
Jessica Kingsley Publishers

Minnie and her dog Max both wish they looked different. When Minnie's Granny sees them both looking glum she brings them for a walk to the park. There they meet loads of dogs and children of all shapes and sizes and they realise that they're all perfect just the way they are.

This book is precious and very clever. Dealing with body image and abilities at the same time in one book is hard, but this one does it brilliantly!

Brontorina
James Howe
Illustrated by Randy Cecil
Acair

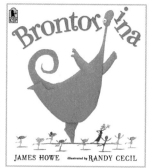

Brontorina has a dream. She wants to dance. But Brontorina is rather large – too large to fit in Madame Lucille's dance studio. Brontorina does not have the right shoes, and everyone knows you can't dance without the proper footwear. Still, Brontorina knows, deep in her heart, that she is meant to be a ballerina.

Body shaming can start at a very young age and it's important to nip it in the bud as soon as possible. *Brontorina* teaches us that nobody needs a 'proper' shape to do what they love, and that determination is the most essential thing.

Independent reader (7–11)

Smile
Raina Telgemeier
Scholastic US

Raina just wanted to be a normal girl, but one night after Girl Scouts she tripped and fell, severely injuring her two front teeth. What follows is a long and frustrating journey with on-again, off-again braces, surgery, embarrassing headgear and even a retainer with fake teeth attached. And on top of all that, there's still more to deal with: a major earthquake, boy confusion and friends who turn out to not be so friendly.

Braces are something that more and more children are having to come to terms with but this book is about so much more than that. Self-confidence can be damaged in so many ways, and the issues raised in *Smile* can help kids dealing with any number of insecurities.

Teen (12–14)

Body Brilliant:
A Teenage Guide to Positive Body Image
Nicola Morgan
Hachette Children's Group

We're all bombarded with information and images – through the media and by our peers – about being too big or too small, being cool, being popular or having the 'right' kind of clothes. This book addresses the body issues that nearly everyone worries about at some point in their lives and gives practical and mindful solutions to work through worries, using real-life examples, quotes and anecdotes from young adults interviewed especially for this book.

A non-fiction title that brings some on-the-nose facts to the situation can be a great help. Making sure a child knows that their feelings are real and important can make all the difference.

Dumplin'
Julie Murphy
HarperCollins Publishers

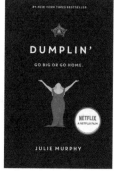

Self-proclaimed fat girl Willowdean Dickson (dubbed Dumplin' by her former beauty queen mom) has always been at home in her own skin. Her thoughts on having the ultimate bikini body? Put a bikini on your body.

When she gets a knock to her confidence she decides to do the craziest thing she can imagine – enter the Miss Clover City beauty pageant – along with several other unlikely candidates – to show the world that she deserves to be up there as much as any girl does.

I love this book (and the Netflix film adaption) so much! The cast of characters who decide to enter the pageant are all shapes and sizes and are proud of it. This is a book about positivity and absolute self-love.

 YA (14+)

Holding Up the Universe
Jennifer Niven
Penguin Books

Everyone thinks they know Libby Strout. Once dubbed 'America's Fattest Teen', she is only seen for her weight, not for the girl underneath. Since her mum's death she's been picking up the pieces in private, along with her heartbroken father. But now, Libby is ready. She's ready for high school, for new friends, for love and for every possibility life has to offer.

Another body-positive novel, this one drives home that everyone has their own insecurities, visible or invisible, and that we all deserve love and acceptance.

Suicide and self-harm

When it comes to discussing someone dying by suicide, it can sometimes be hard to know how much detail to go into when explaining it to children. It is one of the most traumatic and shocking deaths, and although dealing with any sudden death can be hard, there are books geared towards some of the additional feeling that the children and the adults around them might be feeling beyond the grief, that is covered in the bereavement section of this chapter.

I haven't come across any books for very young children that deal specifically with suicide and I think there is a good reason for that. I don't think going into specifics is necessary as we need to protect them from the trauma of such things. Instead, I want to suggest some books that might help a young child deal with the trauma they might experience if they were to find out the circumstances of the death and need help dealing with that. These books can also be applied to other situations as the source of the trauma remains unspecified.

Picture books and independent readers (3–11)

A Terrible Thing Happened
Margaret M. Holmes
Illustrated by Cary Pillo
American Psychological Association

Sherman Smith saw the most terrible thing happen. At first he tried to forget about it, but soon something inside him started to bother him. He felt nervous for no reason. Sometimes his stomach hurt. He had bad dreams. And he started to feel angry and do mean things, which got him in trouble. Then he met Ms Maple, who helped him talk about the terrible thing that he had tried to forget. Now Sherman is feeling much better.

This book is a great discussion starter for any situation where a child has complex feelings after experiencing something traumatic. A lot of the time children don't understand what has happened, so they find it difficult to deal with the feelings attached to it. This book does a great job of helping with that.

The Boy Who Built a Wall Around Himself
Ali Redford
Illustrated by Kara Simpson
Jessica Kingsley Publishers

Boy built a wall to keep himself safe. Behind it he felt strong and more protected. Then Someone Kind came along. She bounced a ball, sang and painted on the other side of the wall, and Boy began to wonder if life on the other side might be better after all.

This book is ideal for a child who has gone through a trauma but didn't get the correct support at the time and has retreated because they can't process what happened.

Teen (12–14)

The List of Real Things
Sarah Moore Fitzgerald
Hachette Children's Group

Grace knows the difference between what's real and the strange ideas that float around in her little sister's mind. Their parents died – that's real. A secret hotel on the cliff-top where their parents are waiting – definitely *not* real. So when grief strikes again, Grace is determined not to let her sister's outlandish imagination spiral out of control. But the line between truth and fantasy is more complicated than it seems ...

Although this is a book about bereavement, it focuses more on how children can hide behind fantasies in an attempt to separate themselves from the trauma in their lives. This book has a wonderful positive outlook and is a great conversation starter for the discussion on different ways to deal with trauma.

▇ *Young Adult (14+)*

It's only really in YA books that we get a true insight into suicide from a young person's perspective. They are old enough to understand and, unfortunately, may need to know the signs of someone struggling. Giving your child one of these books can be an important step in making sure they know that you are there for them and that if they need to talk about what's on their minds, they can come to you.

All the Bright Places
Jennifer Niven
Penguin Books

Theodore Finch is fascinated by death. He's constantly thinking of ways he could kill himself. But each time, something good, no matter how small, stops him.

Violet Markey is waiting for the future. She's counting down the days until she graduates, escapes her Indiana town and her aching grief for her sister's recent death.

When Finch and Violet meet on the ledge of the bell tower at school, they don't know who saves whom.

More Happy Than Not
Adam Silvera
Simon & Schuster

In the months after his father's suicide, it's been tough for sixteen-year-old Aaron Soto to find happiness, but with the support of his girlfriend Genevieve, he's slowly remembering what that might feel like. When Genevieve leaves for a couple of weeks, Aaron starts hanging out with a new guy, Thomas.

Since Aaron can't stay away from Thomas or turn off his newfound feelings for him, he considers turning to the Leteo Institute's revolutionary memory-alteration procedure to straighten himself out, even if it means forgetting who he truly is ...

Mental health

This is an abundant area of publishing as the arts community at large leads the charge in removing the stigma around mental health issues. Whether it is the child who is suffering or someone close to them, it is hugely important that they know to take mental illness as seriously as physical illness. That education can start as young as the picture book age as you encourage children to talk about their feelings and they learn to express themselves openly and confidently.

If you have a teen wanting to start reading around these themes, take your time with them. Books in this area are often visceral and real – reading a few of them in a row can be very draining. For this section, I am just going to put up a general warning: I think these are great books for dealing with the topics but just take it for granted that they are suitable for more mature readers due to the content and topics. Please consider reading a couple of these yourself as teens are more likely to suffer from mental health issues as they move through adolescence, and it is so important that they know you understand and are there if they need to talk.

Picture books (3–7)

The Princess and the Fog
Lloyd Jones
Jessica Kingsley Publishers

Once upon a time, there was a princess. She had everything a little girl could ever want, and she was happy. That is, until the fog came …

Using the fairy-tale structure that children love is a great way to talk about things that can be hard to discuss. This book shows that by talking about problems and getting the right support, every little prince and princess can be made to feel better when foggy thoughts descend!

The Huge Bag of Worries
Virginia Ironside
Illustrated by Frank Rodgers
Hachette Children's Group

Wherever Jenny goes, her worries follow her – in a big blue bag. They are with her all the time – at school, at home, when she is watching TV and even in the bathroom! Jenny decides they have to go, but who will help her get rid of them?

The image of a bag of worries is one with which children will be able to connect instantly. The fun and colourful characters will help take the scariness out of the subject matter and will open the door to a conversation about what's bothering them.

Independent reader (7–11)

Looking After Your Mental Health
Alice James and Louie Stowell
Illustrated by Nancy Leschnikoff and Freya Harrison
Usborne Publishing

We talk about our physical health, but not so much about how we're feeling. With lots of practical advice, this lively, accessible guide explains why we have emotions and what can influence them. Covering everything from friendships, social media and bullying, to divorce, depression and eating disorders, this is an essential book for young people.

This book is accessible and informative, exactly what you need when dealing with such a complex subject. It covers pretty much any topic you could imagine a child would need.

The Unworry Book
Alice James
Usborne Publishing

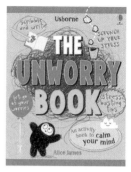

We all worry. This write-in book is an unworry tool-kit, full of things to calm you down and places to put your worries. Activities include creating a worry box, making a mood grid and mindfulness-focused colouring, doodling and mazes. Written with the help of a psychologist, there are links to websites for tips, advice and support.

Sometimes it is just easier and more effective to get things down on paper. This book takes a lot of the advice and science that we need to understand what we are feeling and combines it with activities that really help!

Teen (12–14)

Positively Teenage
Nicola Morgan
Hachette Children's Group

The media often portrays adolescence negatively, but this book shows you how to approach these years far more positively so that you can really flourish and be in control. You'll find simple strategies to develop a positive attitude, growth mindset, self-understanding, determination and resilience and you'll see how those strengths will help you cope with any challenges, enjoy life and achieve your potential.

The teenage brain is not something to trifle with. Understanding how it works and turning it into a book filled with positive messages and advice is no easy feat but this one does it brilliantly.

The Teenage Guide to Stress
Nicola Morgan
Walker Books

This book tackles all the external stresses that teenagers face, including feelings of anger, sadness (and depression), fear of failure, issues caused by changing bodies, body hatred, weight problems, eating disorders and self-harm, pressures of exams and schoolwork, sleep problems, changing relationships with friends and family, boyfriend/girlfriend issues and sexual pressures, bullying and cyber-bullying, as well as other problems arising from the internet.

Although we like to think that the stresses of being a teen are nothing compared to those of being an adult, the reality is that they are just different pressures that are being felt at the same or higher levels. This book does a great job of going through many of these pressures one at a time and giving real advice on how to deal with them.

YA (14+)

Owning It: Your Bullsh*t-free Guide to Living With Anxiety
Caroline Foran
Hachette Books Ireland

Through the filtered lens of social media, it may seem like life's a peach, but for lots of people anxiety is always bubbling beneath the surface. With extensive research and help from the experts, *Owning It* is written with honesty and a bullsh*t-free perspective; consider it your ultimate, practical guide to get you feeling good again.

This book is a mixture of science and advice with effective strategies and activities to help you deal with anxiety issues. Everyone from 14–100 could do with picking this book up!

Bullying

No one wants to think about their child being bullied or even being the bully themselves. Of course parents want everyone to see how amazing and special their children are, just as you see them! Unfortunately, this isn't always the case, so having books on hand with a deep message of kindness and empathy is so important.

Teaching children from a young age that everyone is different and amazing and should be respected means that when they encounter other children they can be considerate while also knowing that if another child is mean to them, it isn't a reflection on them any more than it is on the mean child!

As children get older, understanding how severe bullying can affect self-esteem and mental health in general is of the utmost importance.

If you feel that your child might be having difficulties with bullies in school, sit down and have a real talk about it. Make sure you listen and that you take their feelings seriously. What might seem like a bit of a laugh to you can have deep and dangerous effects on developing minds when they are being subjected to it every day. The books in this section share a theme of empathy and are just as much for parents to read. Understanding what they're going through is the first step in getting them the help they need so they can get back to the extremely important task of being their amazing selves!

Picture books (3–7)

Strictly No Elephants
Lisa Mantchev
llustrated by Taeeun Yoo
Simon & Schuster

When the local Pet Club won't admit a boy's tiny pet elephant, he finds a solution – one that involves all kinds of unusual animals – in this sweet and adorable picture book.

A gorgeous story of acceptance that proves that friends can come in all shapes and sizes and that letting someone new in can lead to loads of new adventures!

Stick and Stone,
Beth Ferry
Illustrated by Tom Lichtenheld
Houghton Mifflin Harcourt Publishing Company

When Stick rescues Stone from a prickly situation with Pinecone, the pair become fast friends. But when Stick gets stuck, can Stone return the favour?

With small children you don't have to worry about being too obvious. This book sends a wonderful anti-bullying message of sticking up for your friends.

Independent reader (7–11)

Wonder
R. J. Palacio
Random House Children's Publishers UK

Auggie wants to be an ordinary ten-year-old. He does ordinary things – eating ice cream, playing on his Xbox. He feels ordinary – inside. But ordinary kids don't make other ordinary kids run away screaming in playgrounds. Ordinary kids aren't stared at wherever they go.

Born with a terrible facial abnormality, Auggie has been home-schooled by his parents his whole life. Now, for the first time, he's being sent to a real school – and he's dreading it. All he wants is to be accepted – but can he convince his new classmates that he's just like them, underneath it all?

This book is a huge bestseller for a reason. It has been translated into over fifty languages and every child and adult should read its message of hope and empathy!

Ella on the Outside
Cath Howe
Nosy Crow

Ella is the new girl at school. She doesn't know anyone and she doesn't have any friends. And she has a terrible secret.

Ella can't believe her luck when Lydia, the most popular girl in school, decides to be her new best friend – but what does Lydia really want? And what does it all have to do with Molly, the quiet, shy girl who won't talk to anyone?

This is an extremely sweet book about a shy child who just wants to fit in. Needless to say, she learns who her friends are and that there is more to life than being popular!

Cover typography – Joel Holland; cover artwork – Nicola Theobald

Teen (12–14)

Blubber
Judy Blume
Pan Macmillan

Blubber is a thick layer of fat that lies under the skin and over the muscles of whales ...

When Linda innocently reads out her class project, everyone finds it funny. Linda can't help being fat, but what starts as a joke leads to a sustained and cruel ritual of humiliation. Jill knows she should defend Linda, but at first she's too scared. When she eventually stands up to the bullies, she becomes their next victim – and what's worse, Linda is now on their side ...

One of the classic anti-bullying books, *Blubber* deals with the complexities of the emotional conflict of wanting to stand up for yourself while also protecting yourself. It reminds us that not everything is black and white when it comes to doing the right thing.

The Harder They Fall
Bali Rai
Barrington Stoke

Cal's family are proud to live in an 'analogue' world – no Wi-Fi in their house, just an ancient black-and-white TV. At school, Cal has no choice but to live in the twenty-first century, coping with a range of bullies and chancers on a daily basis. When Cal's mum decides to 'rebalance' the family with a stint as volunteers at a local food bank, Cal inadvertently discovers new kid Jacob's secret, and Jacob flips.

This book covers a lot, but at its core is standing up for yourself and accepting that not everyone's lot in life is the same.

Used with permission of Barrington Stoke Ltd

■ YA (14+)

Thirteen Reasons Why
Jay Asher
Penguin Books

Clay Jensen comes home from school to find a mysterious box with his name on it outside his front door. Inside he discovers a series of cassette tapes recorded by Hannah Baker – his classmate and crush. Only, she committed suicide two weeks earlier.

On the first tape, Hannah explains that there are thirteen reasons why she did what she did – and Clay is one of them.

This is the toughest one for me to recommend. While I would not give it to a person who's life has been touched by suicide, it is a shocking example of how bullying can come in many different forms. The main character and others around him do not believe that they could have anything to do with the death of a friend but soon come to realise that while they might not have been outright bullies, it doesn't mean they were being kind.

Alternative Families

More and more in modern society we are seeing and celebrating family structures which are outside the normal idea of a 'nuclear family'. Whether it's a child being raised by a grandparent or another family member, a same-sex couple or a parent with a new partner and their own children, we need to be ready to explain how families come in all shapes and sizes but they're all brought together with love.

Not all depictions of non-traditional families are entirely positive in children's books; the trope of the 'evil stepmother' comes to mind, not to mention the Dursleys, Harry Potter's awful aunt and uncle who take him in after the death of his parents.

All too often, the idea of a set of biological parents not raising a child is used as a way to create hardship and pain for the child involved. The books listed here are some among a growing number that show alternative families that are as loving and special as ones that are more typical, even if some of the characters have to get used to the idea.

Same–sex relationships

Picture books (3–7)

And Tango Makes Three
Justin Richardson and Peter Parnell
Illustrated by Henry Cole
Simon & Schuster

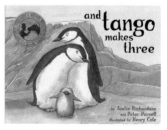

At the penguin house at the Central Park Zoo, two penguins named Roy and Silo were a little bit different from the others. But their desire for a family was the same. And with the help of a kindly zookeeper, Roy and Silo got the chance to welcome a baby penguin of their very own.

This picture book is based on a true story and is as sweet and straightforward as they come! Don't be afraid to use it for slightly older children as well as it is extremely effective at different stages.

. . . .

Mommy, Mama, and Me
Leslea Newman
Illustrated by Carol Thompson
Tricycle Press

Rhythmic text and illustrations with universal appeal show a toddler spending the day with its two mums. From hide-and-seek to dress-up, then bath time and a kiss goodnight, there's no limit to what a loving family can do together.

Mommy, Mama, and Me explores the loving bond between same-sex parents and their children. The beauty of this book is that it's just another sweet picture book which just so happens to feature two mums!

▨ Independent reader (7–11)

The Magic Misfits
Neil Patrick Harris
Egmont UK

This book contains a BIG SECRET. Read on if you dare ...

Do you believe in magic? Carter doesn't. He knows magic tricks are just that – tricks. And as a street magician he's pretty good at them. But then Carter runs away from his conman uncle and he finds himself alone and in danger from dastardly carnival ringleader B.B. Bosso. A chance encounter with the mysterious Mr Dante Vernon leads Carter to a magic shop, where he teams up with five other like-minded kids and the MAGIC MISFITS are born!

The amazingly talented Neil Patrick Harris, who lives with his husband and two children, has written himself into the character of Mr Dante, who runs a magic shop with his husband and daughter.

Teen (12–14)

The Lotterys Plus One
Emma Donoghue
Illustrated by Caroline Hadilaksano
Pan Macmillan

Meet the Lotterys: a unique and diverse family featuring four parents, seven kids and five pets – all living happily together in their big old house, Camelottery. Nine-year-old Sumac is the organiser of the family and is looking forward to a long summer of fun. But when their grumpy and intolerant grandad comes to stay, everything is turned upside down. How will Sumac and her family manage with another person to add to their hectic lives?

This family is as wonderfully tangled as you can get! A brilliant story about intolerance and realising that love and support are the most important things when it comes to family.

YA (14+)

Full Disclosure
Camryn Garrett
Penguin Books

Simone is HIV-positive – and that won't define her. She also knows that celibacy is – technically – the best way to stay safe. Enter Miles Austin: intelligent, funny and way too sexy for Simone to resist. But her classmates don't know that she's HIV-positive – and what is the truth worth in the hands of the wrong person?

Definitely for the older end of the YA scale, but this book delivers! Simone is the adoptive child of two dads who have lived through the AIDS crisis in the US. Their stories lend themselves beautifully to the narrative.

We Are All Made of Molecules
Susin Nielsen
Andersen Press

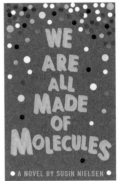

Meet Stewart. He's geeky, gifted and sees things a bit differently from most people. His mum has died and he misses her all the more now he and Dad have moved in with Ashley and her mum.

Meet Ashley. She's popular, cool and sees things very differently from her new family. Her dad has come out and moved out – but not far enough. And now she has to live with a freakazoid stepbrother.

Covering a mix of step-parent and same-sex relationships, this book does a great job of describing a child's feelings when a parent comes out as not straight later in life.

Stepfamilies

Picture books (3–7)

The Family Book
Todd Parr
Little, Brown and Company

The Family Book celebrates the love we feel for our families and all the different varieties they come in. Whether you have two mothers or two dads, a big family or a small family, a clean family or a messy one, Todd Parr assures readers that no matter what kind of family you have, every family is special in its own unique way.

This book fits into most of the categories in this chapter – it's simple yet poignant and shows that all families matter!

The Great Big Book of Families
Mary Hoffman
Illustrated by Ros Asquith
Frances Lincoln Publishers

What is a family? Once, it was said to be a father, mother, boy, girl, cat and dog living in a house with a garden. But as times have changed, families have changed too, and now there are almost as many kinds of families as there are colours of the rainbow!

This is a book every family should have on their shelves. It covers families of all shapes and sizes and is perfect for explaining a specific family type when a child comes home with questions.

Independent reader (7–11)

The Girl With Space in Her Heart
Lara Williamson
Usborne Publishing

Mabel Mynt knows a lot about space ... like how we feel connected to the stars because we are all made of stardust ... and that Mum's new boyfriend, Galactic Gavin, has eyes that twinkle like Sirius, the brightest star in the night sky ... and that sometimes the perfect place for her sister, Terrible Topaz, would be a black hole. But Mabel doesn't know how to fill the space in her heart that Dad left when he walked out. And so she sets out on a mission of discovery ...

This book does a great job of juggling the emotions connected with a step-parent coming into your life and a biological parent leaving. Mix that with a vibrant, fascinating main character and you're really on to a winner with this one!

The Boy Who Sailed the Ocean in an Armchair
Lara Williamson
Usborne Publishing

Becket Rumsey is all at sea. His dad has run away with him and his brother Billy in the middle of the night. And they've left everything behind, including their al-most-mum Pearl. Becket has no idea what's going on – it's a mystery. So, with the help of Billy and a snail called Brian, Becket sets out on a journey of discovery

Teen (12–14)

Step by Wicked Step
Anne Fine
Penguin Books

One stormy night, five stranded schoolchildren uncover the story of Richard Clayton Harwick – a boy who learned many years ago what it was like to have a truly wicked step-father. But the children have stories of their own step-parents to tell – stories that have warmth and humour, as well as sadness, and a fair share of happy endings.

This book is a great conversation starter and because it's aimed at teens, it's a bit darker and not quite as optimistic as the previous titles. This is okay! Stories like these keep them engaged. A few of the stories have happy endings, and I'm sure the kids will see more of themselves in those than the spooky ones.

I Capture the Castle
Dodie Smith
Penguin Books

"I write this sitting in the kitchen sink", is the memorable first line of this enchanting coming-of-age story, told in the form of Cassandra Mortmain's journal. Cassandra wittily describes life growing up in a crumbling castle, with her father who suffers from crippling writer's block, her glam-orous but ineffectual stepmother and her vain but beloved sister Rose. When two visiting Americans arrive, all of their lives are turned upside down, and Cassandra experiences her first love.

This book had to be included because I've never seen love for a book quite like that of one of my best friends for this one. It's a book that demands to be loved with a story that will stay with you. It just so happens to include a 'kooky but loving' stepmother – my friend's words, but I think they're quite fitting.

YA (14+)

Sisters ... No Way!
Siobhán Parkinson
The O'Brien Press

Cindy, a with-it and cynical young teen, still traumatised by her mother's recent death, is appalled when her father falls in love with one of her teachers, a woman with two teenage daughters of her own. Surely he can't be serious? She cannot imagine a worse fate than having a teacher as her step-mother, and as for the two prissy girls – she is never going to call them sisters .... no way!

I adore this book. While a lot of other books deal with the feelings of fear and sadness around a changing family; this one deals with anger. Allowing young adults to know that their feelings are valid is so important and is often the first step towards working through the feelings and coming to a place of understanding and acceptance.

Cover image courtesy of The O'Brien Press Ltd

Alternative parents

Picture books (3–7)

Sometimes It's Grandmas and Grandpas, Not Mommies and Daddies
Gayle Byrne
Illustrated by Mary Haverfield
Abbeville Press

This book shares a child's experience living with and being cared for by grandparents through the eyes of a cheerful and delightful little girl. Poignant moments expressing the child's curiosity and questions give way to comforting and playful exchanges at home with Nonnie and Poppy.

Straight to the point and very sweet, this book is the perfect way to explain to little ones that while their family might be different, they are still loved more than anything!

. . . .

Dennis Lives with Grandma and Grandpa
Paul Sambrooks
Illustrated by Tomasso Levente Tani
CoramBAAF

Dennis the duckling and his sister go to live with their grandparents in a simple story that is easily adaptable to children living in other kinship/ connected person situations, for example, with an aunt, older sibling or close family friend. The story also explores how the decision is made, the ducklings' mixed feelings, and the issue of contact within kinship care, particularly around managing expectations and handling emotions.

Independent reader (7–11)

Race the Atlantic Wind: The Flight of Alcock and Brown
Oisín McCann
The O'Brien Press

In the spring of 1919, after the end of the First World War, teams of pilots and navigators begin to gather on the North American island of Newfoundland. They are attempting what many believe to be impossible – to fly non-stop across the Atlantic Ocean to Ireland. Maggie McRory is a sixteen-year-old girl who sees the gathering of all these aircraft and their crews as a chance to escape her narrow existence.

The Flight of Alcock and Brown

OISÍN McGANN

A thrilling historical novel, this book offers a fantastic insight into the development and dream of long-haul flight. The main character Maggie lives with her aunt and uncle who, like many parents, come into conflict with her dreams.

Cover image courtesy of The O'Brien Press Ltd

. . . .

Check Mates
Stewart Foster
Simon & Schuster

Felix is struggling at school. His ADHD makes it hard for him to concentrate and his grades are slipping. Everyone keeps telling him to try harder, but no one seems to understand just how hard he finds it. When Mum suggests Felix spends time with his grandfather, Felix can't think of anything worse. Granddad hasn't been the same since Grandma died. Plus he's always trying to teach Felix boring chess. But sometimes the best lessons come in the most unexpected of places, and Granddad soon shows Felix that there's everything to play for.

This sweet book is a great example of co-parenting, where the character still has parents in the picture but spends some time living with another family member.

Teen (12–14)

Apple and Rain
Sarah Crossan
Bloomsbury Publishing

Having spent most of her life being raised by her grandmother, when Apple's mother returns after eleven years of absence, Apple feels almost whole again. In order to heal completely, her mother will have to answer one burning question: Why did she abandon her? It's only when Apple meets her younger sister, Rain – someone more lost than she is – that she begins to see things for how they really are, allowing Apple to discover something that might help her to feel truly whole again.

The relationship between Apple and her grandmother is wonderful and real, but when the questions about family circumstances eventually start being asked, it's important to be aware that they stem not from any dissatisfaction with their current guardian, but from a need to know what happened to get them there.

. . . .

Adoption

The finalisation of an adoption is a time of joy and anticipation as a new person becomes an official member of the family. It usually comes following a long-drawn-out process that can leave new parents and their families tired and overwhelmed. When the adoption involves a very young child, it can be a while before the topic of their adoption comes up, but when it does, it is extremely important to broach the subject in the correct way. In the case of children who were adopted older, the system they have gone through may be difficult for them to process and can leave them with feelings of confusion as they try to adjust to a new family. These children might also be dealing with feelings of rejection as they try to understand why they needed to be adopted in the first place.

There are brilliant resources in place to ensure that you and your children are well supported but if you want to open the conversation through books, here are a few options. These can also be helpful if there are biological children or those in the wider family who may need some help understanding the new member and the big changes they bring.

Picture books (3–7)

My Daddies!
Gareth Peter
Illustrated by Garry Parsons
Penguin Books

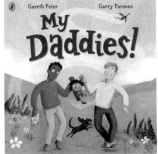

Set off on a series of incredible adventures with an adorable family as the stories they read burst into colourful life. Battle dragons, dodge deadly dinosaurs, zoom to the moon and explore the world in a hot air balloon, before winding down in a wonderfully cosy bedtime ending.

This wonderful book is, of course, one for the same-sex relationship section also, but at its heart is the story of a little girl who loves hearing about the adventure her daddies went on to bring her home. It puts the positivity of adoption and the love of adoptive parents at the centre of the book.

Horton Hatches the Egg
Dr. Seuss
HarperCollins Publishers

On so many levels you can't go wrong with Dr Seuss. Everyone laughs when Horton the Elephant offers to sit on Mayzie Bird's egg while she goes on holiday. What follows is a wacky adventure as Horton does everything he can to look after the egg! This story is a wonderful metaphor for showing that sometimes parents come in all shapes and sizes.

Independent reader (7–11)

Sunny Days and Moon Cakes
Sarah Webb
Walker Books

Little Bird Island has been Sunny's home since she was adopted from China. Sunny loves baking and drawing – if only her anxiety didn't stop her from speaking to her friends. Could a trip to China be the key to unlocking Sunny's voice?

A brilliant story with family love and support at its heart!

The Moon King
Siobhán Parkinson
The O'Brien Press

Ricky has withdrawn from the world into his own inner space. Placed in a foster home which is full of sunshine and goodness, he is uncertain how to become part of family life.

This is a great book to give to children who have been through the foster system or to help other children to understand it.

Cover image courtesy of The O'Brien Press Ltd

· ·

Just Call Me Spaghetti-Hoop Boy
Lara Williamson
Usborne Publishing

Everyone loves superheroes, they solve problems and make people happy, and that's good because Adam's mum needs cheering up. Also, he's found out that before he was adopted his real mum called him ACE. So now he's just got to prove to the world that that's what he is. One mission at a time ...

A fun story with a boy who wants to learn more about where he came from. Suitable for confident readers.

Teen (12–14)

The Story of Tracy Beaker
Jacqueline Wilson
Random House Children's Publishers UK

Tracy is ten years old. She lives in a children's home but would like a real home one day, with a real family.

This is the quintessential teen foster-care book. Wilson is the queen of dealing with difficult topics in a way that really speaks to children on their own level. Not everything always works out for the characters but they know that, even in their disappointment, there are always people ready to look after them.

· ·

Hacker
Malorie Blackman
Random House Children's Publishers UK

When Vicky's adoptive father is arrested, accused of stealing over a million pounds from the bank where he works, she is determined to prove his innocence. But how? There's only one way – to attempt to break into the bank's computer files.

This book is perfect if you're looking for a representation of an adopted child in a thrilling and well-written book. It can be very important to show kids that their circumstances don't define them and that they can have amazing lives that have nothing to do with the difficulties they may have faced before.

 YA (14+)

Goodbye Perfect
Sara Barnard
Pan Macmillan

Eden McKinley knows she can't count on much in this world, but she can depend on Bonnie, her solid, steady, straight-A best friend. So it's a bit of a surprise when Bonnie runs away with a guy Eden knows nothing about five days before the start of their GCSEs. And it's the last person she would have expected.

Sara Bernard is one of my favourite authors and she is quickly becoming the queen of contemporary YA. In this book Eden struggles with keeping a secret from her adoptive parents, who have shown her what family security can look like after a number of years in care with her sister.

Divorce and Separation

The end of a relationship brings with it a huge array of emotions and in many ways is a form of grieving with the same stages as those gone through after the death of a loved one. Trying to mourn the end of the life you thought you were going to have can leave you feeling lost, scared and worried about what the future might bring. This is all even more stressful if there are children in the middle of it all. Trying to explain something that you may not yet have got your head around is no easy task. At the end of the day, the mental and emotional well-being of your children needs to be a priority and you owe it to them to make sure they understand what is happening and that whatever differences you and your partner have, it is not their fault and there was nothing they could have done to change it.

The undercurrent of the list of books in this section is love, because that's what is most important, that your children feel loved and supported and able to explain how they are feeling and that they're being heard. Of course, every situation is different and, depending on the circumstances of the separation, it might be the case that the child is no longer going to see the other parent for their own safety or a variety of other reasons. I've included some books that deal with that scenario too.

Picture books (3–7)

Mum and Dad Glue
Kes Gray
Illustrated by Lee Wildish
Hachette Children's Group

A little boy tries to find a pot of parent glue to stick his mum and dad back together. His parents have come undone and he wants to mend their marriage, stick their smiles back on and make them better.

This is a common feeling for children in this situation but this book teaches that it's not anything the child did which caused the split and that it's not their job to fix it.

Two Homes
Claire Masurel
Illustrated by Kady MacDonald Denton
Walker Books

Alex has two homes – a home where Daddy lives and a home where Mummy lives. Alex has two front doors, two bedrooms and two very different favourite chairs. He has a toothbrush at Mummy's and a toothbrush at Daddy's. But whether Alex is with Mummy or Daddy, one thing stays the same: Alex is loved by them both – always.

This book does a great job of seeing the positives in parental separation. Framing the developments as positives, even when you are feeling the exact opposite, can ensure that children keep a good outlook and just see it as a new adventure.

Raising You Alone
Warren Hanson
Tristan Publishing

A picture book for parents as well as children, this honest and engaging story is the perfect way to say, 'I will always love you'. This book allows the reader to experience single parenting through the eyes of the parent.

This sweet book is another example of using cute animals to deal with a difficult subject, with the parent's love for the child its main message.

Raising You Alone, Copyright © 2005, Warren Hanson. Used with the permission of TRISTAN Publishing, Incorporated.

Independent reader (7–11)

Questions and Feelings About: When Parents Separate
Dawn Hewitt
Illustrated by Ximena Jeria
Hachette Children's Group

This hands-on picture book is designed to help children with their questions and feelings about tricky topics that can be hard to talk about. It offers practical help, tips and advice as well as exploring everyday situations, supported by exquisite and approachable illustrations to give a comforting storybook feel.

The format of this book is perfect for younger but independent readers. It asks children questions after every page and allows them to start processing their feelings. It's also a great chance for you to find out how they are feeling when you may not be sure how to phrase things yourself.

When My Parents Forgot How to Be Friends
Jennifer Moore-Malinos
Illustrated by Marta Fabrega
Peterson's Guides

This sensitively written book assures children that they are in no way responsible for their parents' inability to get along together. It lets kids know that although one parent chooses to move away from the home, both parents continue to love them no matter what.

This very sweet and gentle book is perfect for children who might find the change particularly hard to process. It also encourages children to express how they are feeling to the adult reading the book with them.

Teen (12–14)

Divorce Is Not The End of the World
Zoe and Evan Stern
Tricycle Press

Zoe and Evan Stern know at first-hand how it feels when your parents divorce. When their parents split they knew their lives would change but they didn't know how. A few years later, when they were fifteen and thirteen years old, they decided to share their experience in this positive and practical guide for kids.

It is great to have a book that is written from the child's perspective by the children themselves. It is always helpful to feel that you're not alone and that is at the core of this wonderful book.

The Suitcase Kid
Jacqueline Wilson
Illustrated by Nick Sharratt
Random House Children's Publishers UK

When my parents split up they didn't know what to do with me ... My family always lived at Mulberry Cottage. Mum, Dad, me – and Radish, my Sylvanian rabbit. But now Mum lives with Bill the Baboon and his three kids. Dad lives with Carrie and her twins. And where do I live? I live out of a suitcase. One week with Mum's new family, one week with Dad's. It's as easy as A B C. That's what everyone says. But all I want is to go home – back to Mulberry Cottage ...

Wilson understands how to tackle challenging topics in a way that children will understand without feeling overwhelmed by the heaviness of the character's realities. Andy's feeling of drifting and not knowing where she will land is sure to be shared with many children going through something similar.

■ *YA (14+)*

He Forgot to Say Goodbye
Benjamin Alire Sáenz
Simon & Schuster

On the surface, Ramiro Lopez and Jake Upthegrove couldn't live more different lives. Ram is Mexican-American, lives in the poor section of town and is doing his best to keep his mother sane while his brother fights off a drug-induced coma. Jake is a WASP who drives a nice car, lives in a mansion and has a mother who drinks a bit too much and whose husband, Jake's stepfather, cheats on her.

But there is one point where their lives are exactly the same; their fathers walked out on them when they were just young boys. And at this convergence, Ram and Jake see how everything in their lives is just a little bit similar, because they both blame everything that goes wrong on the one thing they actually have in common.

Books for boys dealing with such emotional topics can be quite difficult to find. This edgy, tough novel deals with feelings of abandonment and what can result from it.

It's Not the End of the World
Judy Blume
Pan Macmillan

Karen couldn't tell Mrs Singer why she had to take her Viking diorama out of the sixth-grade showcase. She felt like yelling, 'To keep my parents from getting divorced!' But she couldn't say it, and the whole class was looking at her anyway.

Karen's world was ending. Her father had moved out of the house weeks before; now he was going to Las Vegas to get divorced, and her mother was pleased! She had only a few days to get the two of them together in the same room. Maybe, if she could, they would just forget about the divorce ...

Getting children to understand that the separation might be the best thing for everyone is hard. A book like this one where the main character tries everything to stop it from happening can show that sometimes staying together isn't the best outcome.

War and the Refugee Crisis

Although we would like to shield children from the scary things in the world, as they go out into it themselves, they will start to encounter people talking about topics they may not understand. Discussions of the refugee crisis and the conflicts that are raging around the world can suddenly land on our doorsteps as more refugees are welcomed into our communities and schools. The children who come from these countries have seen terrible things and have been through more than many of us can even imagine.

Making sure your children have an idea of what their experience might have been means that they can offer a sympathetic ear and make their new friends feel welcomed and listened to. By educating children, you can turn something that is scary and worrying into knowledge that they can use practically outside of the home.

Picture books (3–7)

What is a Refugee?
Elise Gravel
Penguin Books

Who are refugees? Why are they called that? Why do they need to leave their country? In this simple, graphic and bold picture book for young children, author/illustrator Elise Gravel explores what it means to be a refugee. This book is the perfect tool to introduce an important and timely topic to children.

You won't find a more straightforward but also effective book for your very small children. It's perfect if you want to discuss these things in real terms instead of hiding behind metaphors.

Jenny is Scared! When Sad Things Happen in the World
Carol Shuman
Illustrated by Cary Pillo
American Psychological Association

A gentle, comforting, coping story for children who are aware of the threats of violence and terrorism in the world. A range of fears, feelings and questions is explored. Safety, hope and comfort are offered in terms that are honest and reasonable – including the acknowledgement that we cannot control everything.

If you want a book that really speaks to your child and encourages them to talk to you about what's worrying them, then this is the one for you.

Independent reader (7–11)

The Boy at the Back of the Class
Onjali Q. Rauf
Illustrated by Pippa Curnick
Hachette Children's Group

There's a new boy in the class and although he's the same age as everyone else, he's a bit strange. The class aren't sure what to made of him until they find out that he's a refugee who's come from a place full of bombs and fires and other scary things. Can they help him feel welcomed and safe in his new school?

This wonderful book full of empathy does a great job of portraying the horrors of war in a way that children can understand while also making them feel that they can make a difference.

Once
Morris Gleitzman
Penguin Books

For three years and eight months, Felix has lived in a convent orphanage high in the mountains in Poland. But Felix is different from the other orphans. He is convinced his parents are still alive and will come back to get him. When a group of Nazi soldiers come and burn the nuns' books, Felix is terrified that his Jewish bookseller parents will also be in danger.

Aimed at the slightly more mature young reader, this book places them right in the middle of history while also giving an effective insight into what life would have been like for a young Jewish child during the Second World War.

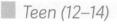

Teen (12–14)

Illegal: One Boy's Epic Journey of Hope and Survival
Eoin Colfer and Andrew Donkin
Illustrated by Giovanni Rigano
Hachette Children's Group

Ebo: alone. His sister left months ago. Now his brother has disappeared too, and Ebo knows it can only be to make the hazardous journey to Europe. Ebo's epic journey takes him across the Sahara Desert to the dangerous streets of Tripoli, and finally out to the merciless sea. But with every step he holds on to his hope for a new life, and a reunion with his sister.

The images of huge numbers of people trying to flee war-torn lands in makeshift boats are frequently in the media. Graphic novels are the ideal way to show the reality of the conditions people endure in their search for safety.

The Diary of a Young Girl
Anne Frank
Penguin Books

In Amsterdam, in the summer of 1942, the Nazis forced thirteen-year-old Anne Frank and her family into hiding. For over two years, they, another family and a German dentist lived in a 'secret annexe', fearing discovery. Anne vividly describes in her diary the frustrations of living at such close quarters, and her thoughts, feelings and longings as she grows up. Her diary ends abruptly when, in August 1944, they were all betrayed.

This is the quintessential text for anyone hoping to really understand the effects of war. A must-read for teens and adults alike.

■ YA (14+)

Children of War: Voices of Iraqi Refugees
Deborah Ellis
Groundwood Books

Deborah Ellis interviewed two dozen young people, mostly Iraqi refugees living in Jordan, but also a few who are trying to build new lives in North America. Their frank and harrowing stories reveal inspiring resilience as the children try to survive the consequences of a war that has nothing to do with them.

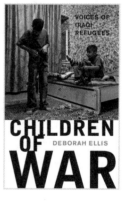

This is tough reading but the stories become so much more real when teens consider that the subjects are the same age as themselves. It's a great book to dip in and out of as there are many different stories in the one volume.

Cover image from Children of War: Voices of Iraqi Refugees copyright © 2009 by Deborah Ellis. Reproduced with permission from Groundwood Books Ltd., Toronto

I Am Malala
Malala Yousafzai
Hachette Children's Group

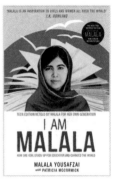

When the Taliban took control of the Swat Valley, one girl fought for her right to an education. On Tuesday, 9 October 2012, she almost paid the ultimate price when she was shot in the head at point-blank range.

Malala Yousafzai's extraordinary journey has taken her from a remote valley in northern Pakistan to the halls of the United Nations. She has become a global symbol of peaceful protest and is the youngest ever winner of the Nobel Peace Prize.

This biography had been re-edited for younger readers, with the more gruesome details omitted and the more complex themes explained. I would encourage you to try to find this edition if you're buying for a young adult.

Life Online

It is fairly common these days to see even small children glued to their phones. Of course there is something to be said for getting kids to put down the devices and pick up a book, but what about using books to help them navigate the online world? The physical world can be a scary place but at least you, and other adults, are able to keep an eye on things and help.

Protecting children when they are online can be a bit of a blind errand as it can be hard to look over their shoulders constantly, especially as they get older. Putting child-protection apps and controls on devices is an essential step to protecting them when they're small, but how do you make sure they take care of themselves as they start taking more independent steps?

The following books help explain that not everything on the internet should be believed –in the same way that you shouldn't trust a stranger on the street, there can also be stranger danger online – and that anything that makes them confused or uncomfortable should be reported to a parent. By doing this, you are making sure that they have a basic knowledge of what is okay and what isn't when they log on to their electronic devices.

Picture books (3–7)

Troll Stinks!
Jeanne Willis
Illustrated by Tony Ross
Andersen Press

Billy Goat and his best friend Cyril are messing about with the farmer's mobile phone, taking selfies and playing games … until they discover the number for a troll. Grandpa Gruff says all trolls are bad, so Billy and Cyril decide to get their own back by sending mean messages. After all, trolls really do stink! Don't they?

A great take on a real issue with a classic fairy-tale structure. Sometimes the best books give their messages without the kids knowing they're getting it!

Chicken Clicking
Jeanne Willis
Illustrated by Tony Ross
Andersen Press

One night Chick hops into the farmer's house and has a browse on his computer – CLICK – soon she's shopping online for the whole farm! But when she arranges to meet up with a friend she's made online, she discovers all is not as it seems …

Online stranger danger is a real issue. Sometimes teaching a lesson through the lens of an animal friend makes it stick a bit more easily with younger readers.

Independent reader (7–11)

Dr Christian's Guide to Growing Up Online
Dr Christian Jessen
Scholastic

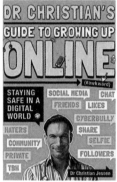

Dr Christian, one of TV's favourite doctor, tackles all your awkward questions head-on, helping you find out how to stay safe growing up in a digital world. From cyber-bullying to binge-watching TV, from group chats to your digital footprint, this book contains REAL answers to REAL questions.

As the kids get a little older, the problems they face online get more complicated too. Make sure to pick this one up yourself if you're getting a bit bogged down in the lingo!

Teen (12–14)

Staying Safe Online
Louie Stowell
Usborne Publishing

The internet is full of amazing possibilities but, just like the real world, there are a lot of potential dangers and difficulties too. You need to know what to watch out for and how to protect yourself. Whether you're worried about oversharing on social media or coming across dangerous people, this guide gives you tips and tools to take control and stay safe online.

This book is particularly good for younger children who are just starting their journey into the online world.

Sex Education

We've seen it played out on TV, in movies and, of course, in books: the adorable little child coming up to a parent asking 'Where do babies come from?' An awkward pause and then some muttering about mummies and daddies who love each other very much usually followed with images of magical birds arriving with babies in colourful blankets.

It's not a straightforward thing to discuss at the best of times and plenty of us even find it hard to talk about these things with other adults. So, when having 'the talk' with kids, there are a few things to keep in mind. Of course, depending on the age the depth of detail you go into will vary dramatically but, as always, there are books for that!

Picture books (3–7)

The best way to engage this age group is to present them with a story that explains the situation with a degree of separation. I don't think we need to get too technical quite yet!

Let's Talk About Girls, Boys, Babies, Bodies, Families and Friends
Robie H. Harris
Illustrated by Michael Emberley
Walker Books

Let's Talk is a fantastic book for very young children on this topic. It goes into enough detail to make children comfortable and engaged but not enough that you have to answer too many follow-up questions.

The New Baby
Anna Civardi
Illustrated by Stephen Cartwright
Usborne Publishing

One of the most common reasons for broaching this subject at such a young age is because a new baby is on the way. Dealing with all of the feelings associated with a new baby can be a challenge.

The New Baby is a very basic book, showing a pregnant woman going into the hospital and coming out with the new arrival. A very positive and sweet book.

Independent reader (7–11)

At this age it's important that you're overseeing what they're reading, so you will still be going through most of their book choices with them.

However, by now they have a better understanding or at least a comprehension of the world around them. Because of this, you need to be ready for them to encounter the world and be ready for the endless questions they are sure to have!

While you can distract smaller children with stories of storks and houses in mummy's tummy, now they're not as easily fooled. As the older end of this age group will also be having sex education in school there's no harm in going through the basics so they're not being introduced to the facts for the first time in front of all of their peers. Just a word of caution - if you do have a basic version of 'the talk' with them, make sure that they know that it's not something they need to tell their friends about. Every family is different and people choose different times to have these conversations, and it's not something that needs to be shouted around the playground. Once again, there are books aimed at presenting the information to younger children.

Let's Talk About Where Babies Come From
Robie H. Harris
Illustrated by Michael Emberley
Walker Books

This does an amazing job of speaking to both children and adults. It breaks down the language barrier that adults might be stuck on when actually faced with trying to explain something that we're very bad at talking about in general. If you're not quite ready to have the talk with your child but you want them to start understanding puberty and what they might expect as they enter their teen years, there are a several books that can be dipped in and out of to explain everything from sex to friendship to hygiene and everything in between. For some children, the idea of their parents talking to them about this stuff is enough for them to sink into the floor with embarrassment.

Teen and YA (12+)

I hope that at this point, thanks to chats with you, classes in school and some books they have read on the topic, your kids are well versed in what they should expect as things start to change. If you're reading this and your child is already in these stages, there are still plenty of books that will speak to them directly as the young adult they are becoming. The two most important things here are that the child has access to information so they can make smart and informed decisions and that they know they can come to you with any questions they might have.

What's Happening to Me?
Usborne Publishing

This book comes in boys' and girls' editions and is a bit more adult in the explanations and portrayal of teen life while presenting it in such a way that this age group can process it.

Consent

Consent at its core is about respect and knowing the difference between when it is given and when it isn't. Young people need to be taught from a young age what consent is so that they can use that knowledge to protect themselves and those around them.

I am not going to go into the details of what constitutes consent, which is a discussion for another book. I offer a guide to books that will help you to start a conversation about consent, whatever the age of your child.

Picture books (3–7)

Let's Talk About Body Boundaries, Consent & Respect
Jayneen Sanders
Illustrated by Sarah Jennings
Educate2Empower Publishing

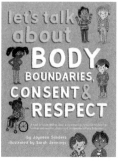

This is perfect for explaining to small children why other people's boundaries are important and must be respected in a friendly and engaging format.

My Body! What I Say Goes!
Jayneen Sanders
Illustrated by Anna Hancock
Educate2Empower Publishing

The crucial skills taught in this book will help children to protect their bodies from inappropriate touch. Children will be empowered to say in a strong and clear voice, 'This is my body! What I say goes!'
A perfect book for slightly older children.

Independent reader (7–11)

Sex is a Funny Word
Cory Silverberg
Illustrated by Fiona Smyth
Seven Stories Press

Much more than a simple facts of life or a 'birds and bees' book, *Sex is a Funny Word* opens up conversations between young people and their caregivers about boundaries, safety and joy.

Teen (12–14)

What Does Consent Really Mean?
Pete and Thalia Willis
Illustrated by Joseph Wilkins
Jessica Kingsley Publishers

'Consent is not the absence of "NO", it is an enthusiastic "YES!!"'

Tia and Bryony haven't considered this subject too seriously until it comes up in conversation with their friends and they realise just how important it is.

This book does an amazing job of introducing the complex ideas that surround the question of consent and provides guidance on how to support someone when they have experienced sexual assault.

What is Consent? Why is it Important? And Other Big Questions
Louise Spilsbury and Yas Necati
Hachette Children's Group

What is Consent? explores how consent works and why it matters. It explains how consent plays a part in almost every interaction or relationship we have, and how it affects almost every area of life, from healthcare to the law. The book encourages children to think about what consent means to them, and about the importance of personal boundaries – knowing your own, and respecting other people's. It talks about how to say no, and what to do if you feel your consent has been violated.

This is a brilliant reference text and is one to have on every teen's bookshelf. It is quite text heavy so it may not be one to sit and read through in one sitting.

YA (14+)

Asking For It
Louise O'Neill
Quercus Publishing

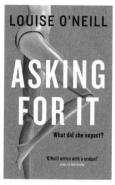

In a small town where everyone knows everyone, Emma O'Donovan is different. She is the special one – beautiful, popular, powerful. And she works hard to keep it that way. Until that night . . . Now, she's an embarrassment. Now, she's just a slut. Now, she is nothing. And those pictures – those pictures that everyone has seen — mean she can never forget.

Definitely a book for more mature readers and their parents, this book shows the stark reality of the rape culture that can be prevalent in the most normal towns and communities.

Inexcusable
Chris Lynch
Bloomsbury Publishing

In a story that moves between the past and the scene of the rape, Keir attempts to defend his character from the monstrous crime of which he has been accused. But the anecdotes from Keir's senior year at high school fall short of giving the innocent, 'good-guy' picture Keir is determined to paint of himself.

Asking for It and *Inexcusable* sit very close to the 'adult' side of young adult. They are very real and can be quite visceral in places. I would recommend reading them yourself so that you are prepared for any questions that may arise. They are extremely important books but please be aware of the seriousness of the content.

Books in Irish

My grasp of the Irish language is tenuous at best. Despite my love of English and reading, languages are not my strong suit! I have many stressful memories of my parents trying to help me with my Irish homework, and I found it really difficult once we started working through full novels in the language.

It's only now that I'm older that I see what a joy it is to be able to converse and share in our native language. It's something I try to work on and I so admire those people who make a point of sharing Irish in their homes outside of schoolwork. If you would like to try to do the same, here are some Irish language books to start with. This is a great way to help support your child's school learning, while also promoting the developmental benefits that come from proficiency in other languages.

As I am in no way an expert in the language, the books that I am recommending here are very much for people who are trying to include more Irish in their lives. I want to try and make this accessible while also acknowledging my own shortcomings, so just look at this as a starting point!

As an aside, you will notice that most of the books I recommend in this section come from Futa Fata. This is a fantastic publishing house who, as well as publishing their own books, also specialise in translating popular brands and authors into Irish. Check out their website for their full range as well as their resources for helping your children to become more comfortable with Irish.

Picture books (3–7)

Cá Bhfuil Puifín Beag?
Erika McGann; Illustrated by Gerry Daly;
Translated by Muireann Ní Chiobháin
The O'Brien Press

A puffling has gone in search of adventure – now her parents can't find her anywhere! Can the animals of Skellig help them find their little puffling?

Cover image courtesy of The O'Brien Press Ltd

Ná Gabh ar Scoil!
Máire Zepf; Illustrated by Tarsila Krüse
Futa Fata

What can a little bear do when he's all ready for his first day of school – but his mother isn't? She sulks, she's shy, she even throws a tantrum. Can Benno convince her that everything's okay? He comes up with an ingenious idea to help her adjust – one that many a mum and dad will recognise.

Independent reader (7–11)

Scuab Fiacal Danny
Brianóg Brady Dawson; Illustrated
by Michael Connor; Translated
by Daire Mac Phaidín
The O'Brien Press

Books like this one from O'Brien Press are a great starting point for independent readers. I have very fond memories of the O'Brien Panda readers and to see so many translated into Irish is fantastic.

Cover image courtesy of The O'Brien Press Ltd

> **TIP:** This brings us to another important tip for children learning Irish as a second language: Don't be afraid to work with a book that was originally published in your first language and then translated. As the list below shows, Irish publishers have been busy snapping up rights deals so some of our favourite brands and books are now available in Irish. Picking a book your child is already familiar with will make the new language less daunting and it means that they can recognise what should be happening in the plot as they read which can help them translate as they go.

Asterix an Gliaire,
René Goscinny; Illustrated by Albert Uderzo; Translated by Antain Mac Lochlainn

Dalen

When Cacofonix the bard is taken to Rome as a present for Julius Caesar, Asterix and Obelix set out to rescue him, sailing with master salesman Ekonomikrisis, the Phoenician merchant. How do our Gaulish friends come to end up training as gladiators?

Dialann Dúradáin
Jeff Kinney
Translated by Máirín Ní Mhárta

Futa Fata

It's a new school year, and Greg Heffley finds himself thrust into middle school, where undersized weaklings share the hallways with kids who are taller, meaner and already shaving. The hazards of growing up before you're ready are uniquely revealed through words and drawings as Greg records them in his diary.

An Cúigear Cróga – Tráthnóna Díomhaoin

Enid Blyton; Illustrated by Jamie Littler; Translated by Máirín Ní Ghadhra

Cló Iar-Chonnacht

It's so terribly hot that the Five are having a lazy afternoon ... but the gang don't get the peace and quiet they imagined! What are the men on the motorbikes up to? Can they be stopped? The classic and beloved Enid Blyton characters are reimagined for a younger audience with full colour illustrations throughout.

Mr Lofa

David Walliams

Translated by Máirín Ní Mhárta

Futa Fata

It all starts when Chloe makes friends with Mr Stink, the local tramp. Yes, he smells a bit. But when it looks like he might be driven out of town, Chloe decides to hide him in the garden shed. Now Chloe's got to make sure no one finds out her secret. And speaking of secrets, there just might be more to Mr Stink than meets the eye ... or the nose.

Teen (12–14)

Maitríóisce

Siobhán Parkinson

Cois Life Teoranta

On Mara's thirteenth birthday her mother gives her a present of Matrioshka dolls from Russia, more a gift for a younger girl, and even then, one of the dolls is missing. When Mara and her friend Dorota go in search of the missing doll they make some discoveries. Mara in particular had no idea of how their lives would change ...

An Táin
Colmán Ó Raghallaigh
Illustrated by Barry Reynolds
Cló Mhaigh Eo

A stunning graphic novel of the Táin, the classic tale of Cúchulainn, Queen Méabh and the cattle-raid for the Brown Bull of Cooley.

Coolbáire
Pádraig Standún
Cló Iar-Chonnacht

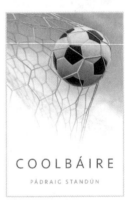

Lorcán Ó Tuathail is eighteen years old and a professional soccer player. Originally from Ireland but living in Spain since he was very young, he's a skilled goalkeeper who plays for one of Barcelona FC's junior teams and is thrilled when he is selected for the senior team. But the reason they moved to Barcelona in the first place was because of his father's criminal activity and involvement in drugs. His father's brothers, a pair of thugs, are taking a special interest in young Lorcán and the gambling opportunities that could make them a lot of money as a result of their nephew playing professionally in La Liga …

Useful Resources for Parents

Parenting

A large part of my job as a children's bookseller was to recommend books to the young people who came in looking for help but, unfortunately, that didn't make me an expert on the children themselves! Many of my customers would also be the parents of those children asking for recommendations for parenting books to help them understand what their child was going through and how they could best help them. This often came from a place of frustration, so if you find yourself angrily going through the shelves in the bookshop looking for something, anything, that will help you understand your little devils/angels do not worry, you are definitely not alone!

Here are my top picks for parenting books to help give you the best insight into the unfathomable place that is your child's mind!

0–6 months

Your Baby Week by Week
Dr Caroline Fertleman and Simone Cave
Ebury Publishing

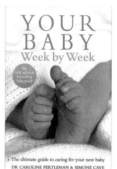

The first six months with a new baby is a special and exciting time full of milestones and new experiences. This updated edition of *Your Baby Week by Week* explains the changes that your baby will go through in the first six months. Each chapter covers a week of baby's development, so you'll know when your baby will start to recognise you, when they'll smile and laugh for the first time and even when they'll be old enough to prefer some people to others!

Toddler

What to Expect: The Toddler Years
Heidi Murkoff and Sharon Mazel
Simon & Schuster

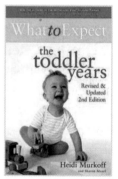

Everyone knows *What to Expect When You're Expecting*, the iconic pregnancy manual. But the other books in the series are great as well.

Overflowing with intelligence and common sense, this comprehensive guide provides clear explanations and useful guidelines on everything a parent might want to know about the second and third years of their child's life. On a month-by-month basis, *What To Expect: The Toddler Years* explains what a toddler will be able to do at that age, and what to expect in the months ahead.

▮ 7–11

How to Talk so Kids Will Listen and Listen so Kids will Talk
Adele Faber and Elaine Mazlish

Piccadilly Press, an imprint of Bonnier Books UK

Parenting experts Adele Faber and Elaine Mazlish provide effective step-by-step techniques to help you improve and enrich your relationships with your children.

Learn how to:
- Break a pattern of arguments
- Cope with your child's negative feelings
- Engage your child's co-operation
- Set clear limits and still maintain good will
- Express your anger without being hurtful
- Resolve family conflicts peacefully

The Whole-Brain Child
Dr Daniel J. Siegel and
Dr Tina Payne Bryson
Little, Brown Book Group

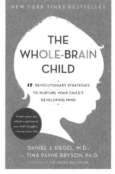

Different parts of a child's brain develop at different speeds and understanding these differences can help you turn any outburst, argument, or fear into a chance to integrate your child's brain and raise calmer, happier children. Featuring clear explanations, age-appropriate strategies and illustrations that will help you explain these concepts to your child, *The Whole-Brain Child* will help them to lead balanced, meaningful and connected lives.

Teen (12–14)

Get Out of My Life ... But First Take Me & Alex Into Town
Tony Wolf and Suzanne Franks
Profile Books

Witty, enjoyable and genuinely insightful, *Get Out of My Life* is now updated with how to deal with everything from social media to online threats and porn, as well as looking at all the difficult issues of bringing up teenagers, school, sex, drugs and more. The message is clear: parenting adolescents is inherently difficult. Don't judge yourself too harshly.

- -

Blame My Brain: The Amazing Teenage Brain Revealed
Nicola Morgan
Walker Books

Contrary to popular (parental) opinion, teenagers are not the lazy, unpleasant louts they occasionally appear to be. During the teenage years the brain is undergoing its most radical and fundamental change since the age of two.

Nicola Morgan's carefully researched, accessible and humorous examination of the ups and downs of the teenage brain has chapters dealing with powerful emotions, the need for more sleep, the urge to take risks, the difference between genders and the reasons behind addiction or depression.

- -

Your child's health and physical well-being

Here are some other books that are helpful for dealing with issues that are more specific and any worries you might be having. Remember, while these books are great references, if you have any worries about your child's health or well-being, contact a professional.

. . . .

When Your Child is Sick: What You Can Do to Help
Professor Alf Nicholson and Gráinne O'Malley
Gill Books

Not intending to be a stand-in for professional medical advice, this book is a great resource to help you understand the basics from first aid to over-the-counter medication. Learning how to treat minor illness at home can reduce your stress as you feel more in control, whatever life might throw at you ... Or what one child might throw at another!

. . . .

The Irish Pregnancy Book: A Guide for Expectant Mothers
Dr Peter Boylan
The O'Brien Press

It's always helpful to have a book that has the healthcare system you are used to as the focus. This book is also particularly helpful as it comes from Dr Peter Boylan, one of Ireland's most experienced and well-known obstetricians.

Cover image courtesy of The O'Brien Press Ltd

. . . .

Dyslexia

There are many resources available for both children and adults with practical advice on how to work with the condition. For specifically Irish help, head to www.dyslexia.ie. This is a great starting point if you're feeling a bit lost and not sure where to get help. There are also a number of chat rooms, forums and Facebook pages where parents come together to help each other out in a safe space.

Because dyslexia is more to do with how the mind processes letters and words, rather than an ability to read, there are loads of practical ways you can tailor the reading experience to the dyslexic mind and help make that processing much easier.

Some of these things might be quite hard to find in most children's books. When you are looking for dyslexia-friendly books find your local stockists of books from Barrington Stoke. This UK publisher prints exclusively dyslexia-friendly books. They also have a range of picture books for adults with dyslexia or who came to reading late, so they can share the joy of reading a book with young children too.

Conclusion

The reason I wrote this book is very simple. Reading and everything that comes with it has given me so much and I wanted to make sure that as many people as possible could share in that. Thanks to my love of reading, I have a career I adore in an industry that is full of the kindest and most interesting people you could ever dream of working with. I have found books to be the great connector as I have built lifelong friendships through our mutual love of getting lost in a world that isn't our own.

Books have given me the courage to believe in myself and my capabilities. They remind me that it is never the characters who have everything from the start who end up making a great story. The best tales are reserved for the underdogs and the downtrodden. Not to mention the quiet people in the back who are waiting for their time to shine or the people who, like me, can't stop talking in case someone might realise that they're not as confident as they try to appear to be.

Whenever I felt overwhelmed or alone, there was always a book ready to help me clear my mind and remind me that even when everything seems lost, there is always hope. There will always be another page, another chapter, or a sequel, and in the end the hard stuff was only there to make the conclusion all the sweeter. Sometimes we need a terrible movie adaption so that we can really appreciate the book it came from.

I hope if you've read this book that it has helped you understand your child a bit better and that you use it to build a stronger relationship between you. No relationship is ever going to be perfect but sometimes that added layer of understanding can help bridge the gap. With the help of books, nothing is unfathomable; it is just all in the delivery. I hope you use the ideas in this book to help your child understand you better; maybe you will allow yourself to be a bit more of an open book so they can learn through you and you can navigate the world together, no matter how different your worlds seem.

Most of all I hope that you help keep the love of books alive in your home, your family and the people you care about. Give and share books as an act of love and care, and there's no limit to what you can achieve.

Acknowledgements

I know it's a cliché to say that your book couldn't exist without the support of other people but I reserve the right to indulge this cliché for the next few paragraphs. I like to joke that this is the closest thing to an autobiography I will ever write because most of the interesting and amazing things that have happened so far in my life have been a result of books and the industry I have been so lucky to work in.

But I must start with my real home and my family. To my parents (to whom the book is dedicated), first of all. Mum, thank you for being my inspiration, for being the person who never would have needed this book and for being the one who taught me that you should never feel embarrassed or stupid for being inquisitive and asking questions (even if plenty of my questions were definitely stupid). Dad, thank you for showing me what passion and dedication look like. You have taught me that if I want to get something done the only barrier is myself and that the naysayers have no place in my head. Tractors and books may be worlds apart, but I have never felt that we are more alike than when I'm starting ten things at once instead of doing the one thing I'm supposed to be doing.

To my brothers Mark and Graham and my (pretty much) sister-in-law Emma, thank you for not slagging me too much when I said I was writing a book. Thank you for showing an interest when I started rabbiting on about things for much longer than was needed. If you zoned out, you were very good at hiding it.

Simon, thank you for being my rock through writing this book. Thank you for insisting we celebrate the little victories as well as the big. Thank you for your patience when I was trying to hit deadlines and for taking my mind off it when I needed a break. You made me feel like I could do anything, and I know I can do anything when you're there to support me.

Thank you to the publishing team at Currach Books, especially Garry and Mags for taking a chance on me and my very basic outline for a book. Thank you to my editor Fiona for being so kind and comforting when I had no idea what to expect from this process and for going easy on me when she sent the dreaded edits. To Michael Brennan, without whom this book never would have existed. I'm sorry for attacking you during a meeting with this idea but I will never regret it!

To my other family in Dubray (Blackrock and beyond), thank you for being the foundation this book was built on. To Mairead for giving me a chance as an overzealous Christmas temp in Grafton Street and Maria for helping me believe that I could build a career in this industry. To Robin, Bobbie, Brian, Ciara, Emmet, Olivia, Shane and Adrian, who were my home away from home and who shared every victory and devastation with me and never let me feel alone. To my regular customers, especially little Catherine, who always reminded me what I was doing it all for. And, of course, thank you to the Dubray children's book buyers who basically taught me most of what I know and who are amazing champions for young readers everywhere.

Thank you to everyone in Penguin Ireland who have been so supportive through this whole process. I started working with them right after I got the deal for this book and they were so excited for me. It is a kindness I will never forget. Thank you to everyone in the sales team – Brian, Carrie, Sophie and Jamie for listening to my rants and reassuring me through this journey.

* * *

Okay, so the friends section is going to be super awkward because I will absolutely miss someone but I will try!

Thank you, Dylan, for always listening to my frustrations and taking them seriously, and Artiola, for cheering me up when things weren't going right. Sophie, your perspective was always valued and I always knew you were on the other end of a text if I got stuck. Eleanor and Jane, thank you for stopping me from pulling my hair out while I finished my edits. Thank you to my book club for still accepting me when I didn't show up for ages because I was working on this, and to Claire for talking to me like I was a real author when I didn't feel like one. To Ryan and Julia Tubridy, Dave Rudden and Sarah Webb, who encouraged me to go for it even when I didn't feel like I was good enough.

Finally, thank you to the children's book industry at large for allowing me to make your world my home. Thank you to the bookshops, libraries and festivals who let me through their doors to do talks and presentations. We in Ireland are so lucky to have such a strong and passionate love for stories and that is never more evident than when we share them with newer generations.